AF522043

FAITH OR AGNOSTICISM

THE FIELD–INGERSOLL DISCUSSION

FAITH OR AGNOSTICISM

American Atheist Press Austin, Texas 1988

The text for this reprint was taken from *Faith or Agnosticism? The Field-Ingersoll Discussion: A Series of Articles from the North American Review (1888)*, E. Haldeman-Julius, ed., booklet B-553 (Girard, Kansas: Haldeman-Julius Publications, n.d.).

American Atheist Press, P O Box 140195, Austin, TX 78714-0195

Published August 1988
Printed in the United States of America

ISBN 0-911826-63-7

Table of Contents

An Open Letter to Robert G. Ingersoll

Dear Sir: I am glad that I know you, even though some of my brethren look upon you as a monster because of your unbelief. I shall never forget the long evening I spent at your house in Washington; and in what I have to say, however it may fail to convince you, I trust you will feel that I have not shown myself unworthy of your courtesy or confidence.

Your conversation, then and at other times, interested me greatly. I recognized at once the elements of your power over large audiences, in your wit and dramatic talent — personating characters and imitating tones of voice and expressions of countenance — and your remarkable use of language, which even in familiar talk often rose to a high degree of eloquence. All this was a keen intellectual stimulus. I was, for the most part, a listener; but as we talked freely of religious matters, I protested against your unbelief as utterly without reason. Yet there was no offence given or taken, and we parted, I trust, with a feeling of mutual respect.

Still further, we found many points of sympathy. I do not hesitate to say that there are many things in which I agree with you, in which I love what you love and hate what you hate. A man's hatreds are not the least important part of him; they are among the best indications of his character. You love truth, and hate lying and hypocrisy — all the petty arts and deceits of the world by which men represent themselves to be other than they are — as well as the pride and arrogance, in which they assume superiority over their fellow-beings. Above all, you hate every form of injustice and oppression. Nothing moves your indignation so much as "man's inhumanity to man," and you mutter "curses, not loud but deep," on the whole race of tyrants and oppressors, whom you would sweep from the face of the earth. And yet, you do not hate oppression more than I, nor love liberty more. Nor will I admit that you have any stronger desire for that intellectual freedom, to the attainment of which you look forward as the last and greatest emancipation of mankind.

Nor have you a greater horror of superstition. Indeed, I might say that you cannot have so great, for the best of all reasons, that you have not seen so much of it; you have not stood on the banks of the Ganges, and seen the Hindoos by tens of thousands rushing madly to throw themselves into the sacred river, even carrying the ashes of their dead to cast them upon the waters. It seems but yesterday that I was sitting on the back of an elephant, looking down on this horrible scene of human degradation. Such superstition overthrows the very foundations of morality. In place of the natural sense of right and wrong, which is written in men's consciences and hearts, it introduces an artificial standard, by which the order of things is totally reversed: right is made wrong, and wrong is made right. It makes that a virtue which is not a virtue, and that a crime which is not a crime. Religion consists in a round of observances that have no relation whatever to natural goodness, but which rather exclude it by being a substitute for it. Penances and pilgrimages take the place of justice and mercy, benevolence and charity. Such a religion, so far from being a purifier, is the greatest corrupter of morals, so that it is no extravagance to say of the Hindoos, who are a gentle race, that they might be virtuous and good if they were not so religious. But this colossal superstition weighs upon their very existence, crushing out every natural virtue. Such a religion is an immeasurable curse.

I hope this language is strong enough to satisfy even your own intense hatred of superstition. You cannot loathe it more than I do. So far we agree perfectly. But unfortunately you do not limit your crusade to the religions of Asia, but turn the same style of argument against the religion of Europe and America, and, indeed, against the religious belief and worship of every country and clime. In this matter you make no distinctions: you would sweep them all away; church and cathedral must go with the temple and the pagoda, as alike manifestations of human credulity, and proofs of the intellectual feebleness and folly of mankind. While under the impression of that memorable evening at your house, I took up some of your public addresses, and experienced a strange revulsion of feeling. I could hardly believe my eyes as I read, so inexpressibly was I shocked. Things which I held sacred, you not only rejected with unbelief, but sneered at with contempt. Your words were full of a bitterness so unlike anything I had heard from your lips, that I could not reconcile the two, till I reflected that in Robert Ingersoll (as in the most of us) there were two men, who were not only distinct, but contrary the one to the other — the one gentle and sweet-tempered; the other delighting in war as his native element. Between the two, I have a decided preference for the former. I have no dispute with the quiet and peaceable gentleman, whose kindly spirit makes sunshine in his home; but it is *that other man over yonder*, who comes forth into the arena like a gladiator, defiant and belligerent, that rouses my antagonism. And yet I do not intend to *stand up* even against him, but if he will only *sit down* and listen patiently, and answer in those soft tones of voice which he knows so well how to use, we can have a quiet talk, which will certainly do him no harm, while it relieves my troubled mind.

What then is the basis of this religion which you despise? At the foundation of every form of religious faith and worship, is the idea of God. Here you take your stand; you do not believe in God. Of course you do not deny absolutely the existence of a Creative Power: for that would be to assume a knowledge which no human being can possess. How small is the distance that we can see before us! The candle of our intelligence throws its beams but a little way, beyond which the circle of light is compassed by universal darkness. Upon this no one insists more than yourself. I have heard you discourse upon the insignificance of man in a way to put many preachers to shame. I remember your illustration from the myriads of creatures that live on plants, from which you picked out, to represent human insignificance, an insect too small to be seen by the naked eye, whose world was a leaf, and whose life lasted but a single day! Surely a creature that can only be seen with a microscope, cannot *know* that a Creator does not exist!

This, I must do you the justice to say, you do not affirm. All that you can say is, that if there be no knowledge on one side, neither is there on the other; that it is only a matter of probability; and that, judging from such evidence as appeals to your senses and your understanding, you do not *believe* that there is a God. Whether this be a reasonable conclusion or not, it is at least an intelligible state of mind.

Now I am not going to argue against what the Catholics call "invincible ignorance" — an incapacity on account of temperament — for I hold that the belief in God, like the belief in all spiritual things, comes to some minds by a kind of intuition. There are natures so finely strung that they are sensitive to influences which do not touch others. You may say that it is mere poetical rhapsody when Shelly writes:

> The awful shadow of some unseen power
> Floats, though unseen, among us.

But there are natures which are not at all poetical or dreamy, only most simple and pure, which, in moments of spiritual exaltation, are almost *conscious* of a Presence that is not of this world. But this, which is a matter of experience, will have no weight with those who do not have that experience. For the present, therefore, I would not be swayed one particle by mere sentiment, but look at the question in the cold light of reason alone.

The idea of God is, indeed, the grandest and most awful that can be entertained by the human mind. Its very greatness overpowers us, so that it seems impossible that such a Being should exist. But if it is hard to conceive of Infinity, it is still harder to get any intelligible explanation of the present order of things without admitting the existence of an intelligent Creator and Upholder of all. Galileo, when he swept the sky with his telescope, traced the finger of God in every movement of the heavenly bodies. Napoleon, when the French savants on the voyage to Egypt argued that there was no God, disdained any other answer than to point upward to the stars and ask, "Who made all these?" This is the first question, and it is the last. The farther we go, the more we are forced to one conclusion. No man ever studied nature with a more simple desire to know the truth than Agassiz, and yet the more he explored, the more he was startled as he found himself constantly face to face with the evidences of MIND.

Do you say this is "a great mystery," meaning that it is something that we do not know anything about? Of course, it is "a mystery." But do you think to escape mystery by denying the Divine existence? You only exchange one mystery for another. The first of all mysteries is, not that God exists, but that *we* exist. Here we are. How did we come here? We go back to our ancestors; but that does not take away the difficulty; it only removes it farther off. Once [you] begin to climb the stairway of past generations, and you will find that it is a Jacob's ladder, on which you mount higher and higher until you step into the very presence of the Almighty.

But even if we know that there is a God, what can we know of His character? You say, "God is whatever we conceive Him to be." We frame an image of Deity out of our consciousness — it is simply a reflection of our own personality, cast upon the sky like the image seen in the Alps in certain states of the atmosphere — and then fall down and worship that which we have created, not indeed with our hands, but out of our minds. This may be true to some extent of the gods of mythology, but not of the God of Nature, who is as inflexible as Nature itself. You might as well say that the laws of nature are whatever we imagine them to be. But we do not go far before we find that, instead of being pliant to our will, they are rigid and inexorable, and we dash ourselves against them to our own destruction. So God does not bend to human thought any more than to human will. The more we study Him the more we find that He is *not* what we imagined Him to be; that He is far greater than any image of Him that we could frame.

But, after all, you rejoin that the conception of a Supreme Being is merely an abstract idea, of no practical importance, with no bearing upon human life. I answer, it is of immeasurable importance. Let go the idea of God, and you have let go the highest moral restraint. There is no Ruler above man; he is a law unto himself — a law which is as impotent to produce order, and to hold society together, as man is with his little hands to hold the stars in their courses.

I know how you reason against the Divine existence from the moral disorder of the world. The argument is one that takes strong hold of the imagination, and may be used with tremendous effect. You set forth in colors none too strong the injustice that prevails in the relations of men to one another — the inequalities of society; the haughtiness of the rich and the misery of the poor; you draw lurid pictures of the vice and crime which run riot in the great capitals which are the centres of civilization; and when you have wound up your audience to the highest pitch, you ask, "How can it be that there is a just God in heaven, who looks down upon the earth and sees all this horrible confusion, and yet does not lift His hand to avenge the innocent or punish the guilty?" To this I will make but one answer: Does it convince yourself? I do not mean to imply that you are conscious of insincerity. But an orator is sometimes carried away by his own eloquence, and states things more strongly than he would in his cooler moments. So I venture to ask: With all your tendency to skepticism, do you really believe that there is no moral government of the world — no Power behind nature "making for righteousness"? Are there no retributions in history? When Lincoln stood on the field of Gettysburg so lately drenched with blood, and, reviewing the carnage of that terrible day, accepted it as the punishment of our national sins, was it a mere theatrical flourish in him to lift his hand to heaven, and exclaim, "Just and true are Thy ways, Lord

God Almighty!"

Having settled it to your own satisfaction that there is no God, you proceed in the same easy way to dispose of that other belief which lies at the foundation of all religion — the immortality of the soul. With an air of modesty and diffidence that would carry an audience by storm, you confess your ignorance of what, perhaps, others are better acquainted with, when you say, "This world is all that *I* know anything about, *so far as I recollect.*" This is very wittily put, and some may suppose it contains an argument; but do you really mean to say that you do not *know* anything except what you "recollect" or what you have seen with your eyes? Perhaps you never saw your grandparents, but have you any more doubt of their existence than of that of your father and mother whom you did see?

Here, as when you speak of the existence of God, you carefully avoid any positive affirmation: you neither affirm nor deny. You are ready for whatever may "turn up." In your jaunty style, if you find yourself hereafter in some new and unexpected situation, you will accept it and make the best of it and be "as ready as the next man to enter on any remunerative occupation!"

But while airing this pleasant fancy, you plainly regard the hope of another life as a beggar's dream — the momentary illusion of one who, stumbling along life's highway, sets him down by the roadside, footsore and weary, cold and hungry, and falls asleep, and dreams of a time when he shall have riches and plenty. Poor creature! let him dream; it helps him to forget his misery and may give him a little courage for his rude awakening to the hard reality of life. But it is all a dream, which dissolves in thin air, and floats away and disappears. This illustration I do not take from you but simply choose to set forth what (as I infer from the sentences above quoted and many like expressions) may describe, not unfairly, your state of mind. Your treatment of the subject is one of trifling. You do not speak of it in a serious way, but lightly and flippantly, as if it were all a matter of fancy and conjecture, and not worthy of sober consideration.

Now, does it never occur to you that there is something very cruel in this treatment of the belief of your fellow-creatures, on whose hope of another life hangs all that relieves the darkness of their present existence? To many of them life is a burden to carry, and they need all the helps to carry it that can be found in reason, in philosophy, or in religion. But what support does your hollow creed supply? You are a man of warm heart, of the tenderest sympathies. Those who know you best, and love you most, tell me that you cannot bear the sight of suffering even in animals; that your natural sensibility is such that you find no pleasure in sports, in hunting or fishing; to shoot a robin would make you feel like a murderer. If you see a poor man in trouble your first impulse is to help him. You cannot see a child in tears but you want to take up the little fellow in your arms, and make him smile again. And yet, with all your sensibility, you hold the most remorseless and pitiless creed in the world — a creed in which there is not a gleam of mercy or of hope. A mother has lost her only son. She goes to his grave and throws herself upon it, the very picture of woe. One thought only keeps her from despair: it is that beyond this life there is a world where she may once more clasp her boy in her arms. What will you say to that mother? You are silent, and your silence is a sentence of death to her hopes. By that grave you cannot speak, for if you were to open your lips and tell that mother what you really believe, it would be that her son is blotted out of existence, and that she can never look upon his face again. Thus with your iron heel do you trample down and crush the last hope of a broken heart.

When such sorrow comes to you, you feel it as keenly as any man. With your strong domestic attachments one cannot pass out of your little circle without leaving a great void in your heart, and your grief is as eloquent as it is hopeless. No sadder words ever fell from human lips than these, spoken over the coffin of one to whom you were tenderly attached: "Life is but a narrow vale, between the cold and barren peaks of two eternities!" This is a doom of annihilation, which strikes a chill to the stoutest heart. Even you must envy the faith which, as it looks upward, sees those "peaks of two eternities," not "cold and barren," but warm with the glow of the setting sun, which gives promise of a happier tomorrow!

I think I hear you say, "So might it be! Would that I could believe it!" for no one recognizes more the emptiness of life as it is. I do not forget the tone in which you said: "Life is very sad to me; it is very pitiful; there isn't much to it." True indeed! With your belief, or want of belief, there is very little to it; and if this were all, it would be a fair question whether life were worth living. In the name of humanity, let us cling to all that is left us that can bring a ray of hope into its darkness, and thus lighten its otherwise impenetrable gloom.

I observe that you not infrequently entertain yourself and your audiences by caricaturing certain doctrines of the Christian religion. The "Atonement," as you look upon it, is simply "punishing the wrong man" — letting the guilty escape and putting the innocent to death. This is vindicating justice by permitting injustice. But is there not another side to this? Does not the idea of sacrifice run through human life, and ennoble human character? You see a mother denying herself for her children, foregoing every comfort, enduring every hardship, till at last, worn out by her labor and her privation, she folds her hands upon her breast. May it not be said truly that she *gives her life* for the life of her children? History is full of sacrifice, and it is the best part of history. I will not speak of "the noble army of martyrs," but of heroes who have died for their country or for liberty — what is it but this element of devotion for the good of others that gives such glory to their immortal names? How then should it be thought a thing without reason that a Deliverer of the race should give His life for the life of the world?

So, too, you find a subject for caricature in the doctrine of "Regeneration." But what is regeneration but a change of character shown in a change of life? Is that so very absurd? Have you never seen a drunkard reformed? Have you never seen a man of impure life, who, after running his evil course, had, like the prodigal, "come to himself" — that is, awakened to his shame, and turning from it, come back to the path of purity, and finally regained a true and noble manhood? Probably you would admit this, but say that the change was the result of reflection, and of the man's own strength of will. The doctrine of regeneration only adds to the will of man the power of God. We believe that man is weak, but that God is mighty; and that when man tries to raise himself, an arm is stretched out to lift him up to a height which he could not attain alone. Sometimes one who has led the worst life, after being plunged into such remorse and despair that he feels as if he were enduring the agonies of hell, turns back and takes another course: he becomes "a new creature," whom his friends can hardly recognize as he "sits clothed and in his right mind." The change is from darkness to light, from death to life; and he who has known but one such case will never say that the language is too strong which describes that man as "born again."

If you think that I pass lightly over these doctrines, not bringing out all the meaning which they bear, I admit it. I am not writing an essay in theology, but would only show, in passing, by your favorite method of illustration, that the principles involved are the same with which you are familiar in everyday life.

But the doctrine which excites your bitterest animosity is that of Future Retribution. The prospect of another life, reaching on into an unknown futurity, you would contemplate with composure were it not for the dark shadow hanging over it. But to live only to suffer; to live when asking to die; to "long for death, and not be able to find it" —

is a prospect which arouses the anger of one who would look with calmness upon death as an eternal sleep. The doctrine loses none of its terrors in passing through your hands; for it is one of the means by which you work upon the feelings of your hearers. You pronounce it "the most horrible belief that ever entered the human mind: that the Creator should bring beings into existence to destroy them! This would make Him the most fearful tyrant in the universe — a Moloch devouring his own children!" I shudder when I recall the fierce energy with which you spoke as you said, "Such a God I hate with all the intensity of my being!"

But gently, gently, Sir! We will let this burst of fury pass before we resume the conversation. When you are a little more tranquil, I would modestly suggest that perhaps you are fighting a figment of your imagination. I never heard of any Christian teacher who said that "the Creator brought beings into the world to destroy them!" Is it not better to moderate yourself to exact statements, especially when, with all modifications, the subject is one to awaken a feeling the most solemn and profound?

Now I am not going to enter into a discussion of this doctrine. I will not quote a single text. I only ask you whether it is not a scientific truth that *the effect of everything which is of the nature of a cause is eternal.* Science has opened our eyes to some very strange facts in nature. The theory of vibrations is carried by the physicists to an alarming extent. They tell us that it is literally and mathematically true that you cannot throw a ball in the air but it shakes the solar system. Thus all things act upon all. What is true in space may be true in time, and the law of physics may hold in the spiritual realm. When the soul of man departs out of the body, being released from the grossness of the flesh, it may enter on a life a thousand times more intense than this: in which it will not need the dull senses as avenues of knowledge, because the spirit itself will be all eye, all ear, all intelligence; while memory, like an electric flash, will in an instant bring the whole of the past into view; and the moral sense will be quickened as never before. Here then we have all the conditions of retribution — a world which, however shadowy it may seem, is yet as real as the homes and habitations and activities of our present state; with memory trailing the deeds of a lifetime behind it, and conscience, more inexorable than any judge, giving its solemn and final verdict.

With such conditions assumed, let us take a case which would awaken your just indignation — that of a selfish, hardhearted, and cruel man; who sacrifices the interests of everybody to his own; who grinds the faces of the poor, robbing the widow and the orphan of their little all; and who, so far from making restitution, dies with his ill-gotten gains held fast in his clenched hand. How long must the night be to sleep away the memory of such a hideous life? If he wakes, will not the recollection cling to him still? Are there any waters of oblivion that can cleanse his miserable soul? If not — if he cannot *forget* — surely he cannot *forgive* himself for the baseness which now he has no opportunity to repair. Here, then, is a retribution which is inseparable from his being, which is a part of his very existence. The undying memory brings the undying pain.

Take another case — alas! too sadly frequent. A man of pleasure betrays a young, innocent, trusting woman by the promise of his love, and then casts her off, leaving her to sink down, down, through every degree of misery and shame, till she is lost in depths, which plummet never sounded, and disappears. Is he not to suffer for this poor creature's ruin? Can he rid himself of it by fleeing beyond "that bourne from whence no traveler returns"? Not unless he can flee from himself: for in the lowest depths of the under-world — a world in which the sun never shines — that image will still pursue him. As he wanders in its gloomy shades a pale form glides by him like an affrighted ghost. The face is the same, beautiful even in its sorrow, but with a look upon it as of one who has already suffered an eternity of woe. In an instant all the past comes back again. He sees the young, unblessed mother wandering in some lonely place, that only the heavens may witness her agony and her despair. There he sees her holding up in her arms the babe that had no right to be born, and calling upon God to judge her betrayer. How far in the future must he travel to forget that look? Is there any escape except by plunging into the gulf of annihilation?

Thus far in this paper I have taken a tone of defence. But I do not admit that the Christian religion needs any apology, — it needs only to be rightly understood to furnish its own complete vindication. Instead of considering its "evidences," which is but going round the outer walls, let us enter the gates of the temple and see what is within. Here we find something better than "towers and bulwarks" in the character of Him who is the Founder of our Religion, and not its Founder only, but its very core and being. Christ *is* Christianity. Not only is He the Great Teacher, but the central subject of what He taught, so that the whole stands or falls with Him.

In our first conversation, I observed that, with all your sharp comments on things sacred, you professed great respect for the ethics of Christianity, and for its author. "Make the Sermon on the Mount your religion," you said, "and there I am with you." Very well! So far, so good. And now, if you will go a little further, you may find still more food for reflection.

All who have made a study of the character and teachings of Christ, even those who utterly deny the supernatural, stand in awe and wonder before the gigantic figure which is here revealed. Renan closes his "Life of Jesus" with this as the result of his long study: "Jesus will never be surpassed. His worship will be renewed without ceasing; his story [legende] will draw tears from beautiful eyes without end; his sufferings will touch the finest natures; *all the ages will proclaim that among the sons of men there has not risen a greater than Jesus;*" while Rousseau closes his immortal eulogy by saying, "*Socrates died like a philosopher, but Jesus Christ like a God!*"

Here is an argument for Christianity to which I pray you to address yourself. As you do not believe in miracles, and are ready to explain everything by natural causes, I beg you to tell us how came it to pass that a Hebrew peasant, born among the hills of Judea, had a wisdom above that of Socrates or Plato, of Confucious or Buddha? This is the greatest of miracles, that such a Being has lived and died on the earth.

Since this is the chief argument for Religion, does it not become one who undertakes to destroy it to set himself first to this central position, instead of wasting his time on mere outposts? When you next address one of the great audiences that hang upon your words, is it unfair to ask that you lay aside such familiar topics as Miracles or Ghosts, or a reply to Talmage, and tell us what you think of *Jesus Christ*; whether you look upon Him as an impostor, or merely as a dreamer — a mild and harmless enthusiast; or are you ready to acknowledge that He is entitled to rank among the great teachers of mankind?

But if you are compelled to admit the greatness of Christ, you take your revenge on the Apostles, whom you do not hesitate to say that you "don't think much of." In fact, you set them down in a most peremptory way as "a poor lot." It did seem rather an unpromising "lot," that of a boat-load of fishermen, from which to choose the apostles of a religion — almost as unpromising as it was to take a rail-splitter to be the head of a nation in the greatest crisis of its history! But perhaps in both cases there was a wisdom higher than ours, that chose better than we. It might puzzle even you to give a better definition of religion than this of the Apostle James: "Pure religion and undefiled before God and the Father is this: to visit the fatherless and widows in their affliction, and to keep himself unspotted from the world;" or to find among those sages of antiquity, with whose writings you are familiar, a more complete and perfect delineation of that which is the essence of all goodness and virtue, than Paul's description of the charity which "suffereth long and is kind;" or to find in the sayings of Confucious or of Buddha anything more sublime than this aphorism of John: "God is love, and he that dwelleth in love dwelleth in God, and God in him."

And here you must allow me to make a remark, which is not intended as a personal retort, but simply in the interest of that truth which we both profess to seek, and to count worth more than victory. Your language is too sweeping to indicate the careful thinker, who measures his words and weighs them in a balance. Your lectures remind me of the pictures of Gustave Doré, who preferred to paint on a large canvas, with figures as gigantesque as those of Michael Angelo in his Last Judgment. The effect is very powerful, but if he had softened his colors a little — if there were a few delicate touches, a mingling of light and shade, as when twilight is stealing over the earth, — the landscape would be more true to nature. So, believe me, your words would be more weighty if they were not so strong. But whenever you touch upon religion you seem to lose control of yourself, and a vindictive feeling takes possession of you, which causes you to see things so distorted from their natural appearance that you cannot help running into the broadest caricature. You swing your sentences as the woodman swings his axe. Of course, this "slashing" style is very effective before a popular audience, which does not care for nice distinctions, or for evidence that has to be sifted and weighed; but wants opinions off hand, and likes to have its prejudices and hatreds echoed back in a ringing voice. This carries the crowd, but does not convince the philosophic mind. The truth-seeker cannot cut a road through the forest with sturdy blows; he has a hidden path to trace, and must pick his way with slow and cautious step to find that which is more precious than gold.

But if it were possible for you to sweep away the "evidences of Christianity," you have not swept away Christianity itself; it still lives, not only in tradition, but in the hearts of the people, entwined with all that is sweetest in their domestic life, from which it must be torn out with unsparing hand before it can be exterminated. To begin with, you turn your back upon history. All that men have done and suffered for the sake of religion was folly. The Pilgrims, who crossed the sea to find freedom to worship God in the forests of the New World, were miserable fanatics. There is no more place in the world for heroes and martyrs. He who sacrifices his life for a faith, or an idea, is a fool. The only practical wisdom is to have a sharp eye to the main chance. If you keep on in this work of demolition, you will soon destroy all our ideals. Family life withers under the cold sneer — half pity and half scorn — with which you look down on household worship. Take from our American firesides such scenes as that pictured in the *Cotter's Saturday Night,* and you have taken from them their most sacred hours and their tenderest memories.

The same destructive spirit which intrudes into our domestic, as well as our religious life, would take away the beauty of our villages as well as the sweetness of our homes. In the weary round of a week of toil, there comes an interval of rest; the laborer lays down his burden, and for a few hours breathes a serener air. The Sabbath morning has come:

Sweet day! so cool, so calm, so bright,
The bridal of the earth and sky.

At the appointed hour the bell rings across the valley, and sends its echoes among the hills; and from all the roads the people come trooping to the village church. Here they gather, old and young, rich and poor; and as they join in the same act of worship, feel that God is the maker of them all? Is there in our national life any influence more elevating than this — one which tends more to bring a community together; to promote neighborly feeling; to refine the manners of the people; to breed true courtesy, and all that makes a Christian village different from a cluster of Indian wigwams — a civilized community different from a tribe of savages?

All this you would destroy: you would abolish the Sabbath, or have it turned into a holiday; you would tear down the old church, so full of tender associations of the living and the dead, or at least have it "razeed," cutting off the tall spire that points upward to heaven; and the interior you would turn into an Assembly room — a place of entertainment, where the young people could have their merry-makings, except perchance in the warm Summer-time, when they could dance on the village green! So far you would have gained your object. But would that be a more orderly community, more refined or more truly happy?

You may think this a mere sentiment — that we care more for the picturesque than for the true. But there is one result which is fearfully real: the destructive creed, or no creed, which despoils our churches and our homes, attacks society in its first principles by taking away the support of morality. I do not believe that general morality can be upheld without the sanctions of religion. There may be individuals of great natural force of character, who can stand alone — men of superior intellect and strong will. But in general human nature is weak, and virtue is not the spontaneous growth of childish innocence. Men do not become pure and good by instinct. Character, like mind, has to be developed by education; and it needs all the elements of strength which can be given it, from without as well as from within, from the government of man and the government of God. To let go of these restraints is a peril to public morality.

You feel strong in the strength of a robust manhood, well poised in body and mind, and in the centre of a happy home, where loving hearts cling to you like vines round the oak. But many to whom you speak are quite otherwise. You address thousands of young men who have come out of country homes, where they have been brought up in the fear of God, and have heard the morning and evening prayer. They come into a city full of temptations, but are restrained from evil by the thought of father and mother, and reverence for Him who is the Father of us all — a feeling which, though it may not have taken the form of any profession, is yet at the bottom of their hearts, and keeps them from many a wrong and wayward step. A young man, who is thus "guarded and defended" as by unseen angels, some evening when he feels very lonely, is invited to "go and hear Ingersoll," and for a couple of hours listens to your caricatures of religion, with descriptions of the prayers and the psalm-singing, illustrated by devout grimaces and nasal tones, which set the house in roars of laughter, and are received with tumultuous applause. When it is all over, and the young man finds himself again under the flaring lamps of the city streets, he is conscious of a change; the faith of his childhood has been rudely torn from him, and with it "a glory has passed away from the earth;" the Bible which his mother gave him, the morning that he came away, is "a mass of fables;" the sentence which she wished him to hang on the wall, "Thou, God, seest me," has lost its power, for there is no God that sees him, no moral government, no law and no retribution. So he reasons as he walks slowly homeward, meeting the temptations which haunt these streets at night — temptations from which he has hitherto turned with a shudder, but which he now meets with a diminished power of resistance. Have you done that young man any good in taking from him what he held sacred before? Have you not left him morally weakened? From sneering at religion, it is but a step to sneering at morality, and then but one step more to a vicious and profligate career. How are you going to stop this downward tendency? When you have stripped him of former restraints, do you leave him anything in their stead, except indeed a sense of honor, self-respect, and self-interest? — worthy motives, no doubt, but all too feeble to withstand the fearful temptations that assail him. Is the chance of his resistance as good as it was before? Watch him as he goes along that street at midnight! He passes by the places of evil resort, of drinking and gambling — those open mouths of hell; he hears the sound of music and dancing, and for the first time pauses to listen. How long will it be before he will venture in?

With such dangers in his path, it is a grave responsibility to loosen the restraints which hold such a young man to virtue. These gibes and sneers which you utter so lightly, may have a sad echo in a lost character and a wretched life. Many a young man has been thus taunted until he has pushed off from the shore, under the idea of gaining his "liberty," and ventured into the rapids, only to be carried down the stream, and left a wreck in the whirlpool below.

You tell me that your object is to drive fear out of the world. That is a noble ambition; if you succeed, you will be indeed a deliverer. Of course you mean only irrational fears. You would not have men throw off the fear of violating the laws of nature; for that would lead to incalculable misery. You aim only at the terrors born of ignorance and superstition. But how are you going to get rid of these? You trust to the progress of science, which has dispelled so many fears arising from physical phenomena, by showing that calamities ascribed to spiritual agencies are explained by natural causes. But science can only go a certain way, beyond which we come into the sphere of the unknown, where all is dark as before. How can you relieve the fears of others — indeed how can you rid yourself of fear, believing as you do that there is no Power above which can help you in any extremity; that you are the sport of accident, and may be dashed in pieces by the blind agency of nature? If I believed this, I should feel that I was in the grasp of some terrible machinery which was crushing me to atoms, with no possibility of escape.

Not so does Religion leave man here on the earth, helpless and hopeless — in abject terror, as he is in utter darkness as to his fate — but opening the heaven above him, it discovers a Great Intelligence, compassing all things, seeing the end from the beginning, and ordering our little lives so that even the trials that we bear, as they call out the finer elements of character, conduce to our future happiness. God is our Father. We look up into His face with childlike confidence, and find that "His service is perfect freedom." "Love casts out fear." That, I beg to assure you, is the way, and the only way, by which man can be delivered from those fears by which he is all his lifetime subject to bondage.

In your attacks upon Religion you do violence to your own manliness. Knowing you as I do, I feel sure that you do not realize where your blows fall, or whom they wound, or you would not use your weapons so freely. The faiths of men are as sacred as the most delicate manly or womanly sentiments of love and honor. They are dear as the beloved faces that have passed from our sight. I should think myself wanting in respect to the memory of my father and mother if I could speak lightly of the faith in which they lived and died. Surely this must be mere thoughtlessness, for I cannot believe that you find pleasure in giving pain. I have not forgotten the gentle hand that was laid upon your shoulder, and the gentle voice which said, "Uncle Robert wouldn't hurt a fly." And yet you bruise the tenderest sensibilities, and trample down what is most cherished by millions of sisters and daughters and mothers, little heeding that you are sporting with "human creatures' lives."

You are waging a hopeless war — a war in which you are certain only of defeat. The Christian Religion began to be nearly two thousand years before you and I were born, and it will live two thousand years after we are dead. Why is it that it lives on and on, while nations and kingdoms perish? Is not this "the survival of the fittest"? Contend against it with all your wit and eloquence, you will fail, as all have failed before you. You cannot fight against the instincts of humanity. It is as natural for men to look up to a Higher Power as it is to look up to the stars. Tell them that there is no God! You might as well tell them that there is no Sun in heaven, even while on that central light and heat all life on earth depends.

I do not presume to think that I have convinced you, or changed your opinion; but it is always right to appeal to a man's "sober second thought" — to that better judgment that comes with increasing knowledge and advancing years, and I will not give up hope that you will yet see things more clearly, and recognize the mistake you have made in not distinguishing Religion from Superstition — two things as far apart as "the hither from the utmost pole." Superstition is the greatest enemy of Religion. It is the nightmare of the mind, filling it with all imaginable terrors — a black cloud which broods over half the world. Against this you may well invoke the light of science to scatter its darkness. Whoever helps to sweep it away, is a benefactor of his race. But when this is done, and the moral atmosphere is made pure and sweet, then you as well as we may be conscious of a new Presence coming into the hushed and vacant air, as Religion, daughter of the skies, descends to earth to bring peace and good will to men.

Henry M. Field

A Reply to the Rev. Henry M. Field, D.D.

"Doubt is called the beacon of the wise."

My Dear Mr. Field:

I answer your letter because it is manly, candid and generous. It is not often that a minister of the gospel of universal benevolence speaks of an unbeliever except in terms of reproach, contempt and hatred. The meek are often malicious. The statement in your letter, that some of your brethren look upon me as a monster on account of my unbelief, tends to show that those who love God are not always the friends of their fellow men.

Is it not strange that people who admit that they ought to be eternally damned, that they are by nature totally depraved, and that there is no soundness or health in them, can be so arrogantly egotistic as to look upon others as "monsters"? And yet "some of your brethren," who regard unbelievers as infamous, rely for salvation entirely on the goodness of another, and expect to receive as alms an eternity of joy.

The first question that arises between us, is as to the innocence of honest error — as to the right to express an honest thought.

You must know that perfectly honest men differ on many important subjects. Some believe in free trade, others are the advocates of protection. There are honest Democrats and sincere Republicans. How do you account for these differences? Educated men, presidents of colleges, cannot agree upon questions capable of solution — questions that the mind can grasp, concerning which the evidence is open to all and where the facts can be with accuracy ascertained. How do you explain this? If such differences can exist consistently with the good faith of those who differ, can you not conceive of honest people entertaining different views on subjects about which nothing can be positively known?

You do not regard me as a monster. "Some of your brethren" do. How do you account for this difference? Of course, your brethren — their hearts having been softened by the Presbyterian God — are governed by charity and love. They do not regard me as a monster because I have committed an infamous crime, but simply for the reason that I have expressed my honest thoughts.

What should I have done? I have read the Bible with great care, and the conclusion has forced itself upon my mind not only that it is not inspired, but that it is not true. Was it my duty to speak or act contrary to this conclusion? Was it my duty to remain silent? If I had been untrue to myself, if I had joined the majority, — if I had declared the book to be the inspired word of God, — would your brethren still have regarded me as a monster? Has religion had control of the world so long that an honest man seems monstrous?

According to your creed — according to your Bible — the same Being, who made the mind of man, who fashioned every brain, and sowed within those wondrous fields the seeds of every thought and deed, inspired the Bible's every word, and gave it as a guide to all the world. Surely the book should satisfy the brain. And yet, there are millions who do not believe in the inspiration of the Scriptures. Some of the greatest and best have held the claim of inspiration in contempt. No Presbyterian ever stood higher in the realm of thought than Humboldt. He was familiar with Nature from sands to stars, and gave his thoughts, his discoveries and conclusions, "more precious than the tested gold," to all mankind. Yet he not only rejected the religion of your brethren, but denied the existence of their God. Certainly, Charles Darwin was one of the greatest and purest of men, — as free from prejudice as the mariner's compass, — desiring only to find amid the mists and clouds of ignorance the star of truth. No man ever exerted a greater influence on the intellectual world. His discoveries, carried to their legitimate conclusion, destroy the creeds and sacred Scriptures of mankind. In the light of "Natural Selection," "The Survival of the Fittest," and "The Origin of Species," even the Christian religion becomes a gross and cruel superstition. Yet Darwin was an honest, thoughtful, brave and generous man.

Compare, I beg of you, these men, Humboldt and Darwin, with the founders of the Presbyterian Church. Read the life of Spinoza, the loving pantheist, and then that of John Calvin, and tell me, candidly, which, in your opinion, was a "monster." Even your brethren do not claim that men are to be eternally punished for having been mistaken as to the truths of geology, astronomy, or mathematics. A man may deny the rotundity and rotation of the earth, laugh at the attraction of gravitation, scout the nebular hypothesis, and hold the multiplication table in abhorrence, and yet join at last the angelic choir. I insist upon the same freedom of thought in all departments of human knowledge. Reason is the supreme and final test.

If God has made a revelation to man, it must have been addressed to his reason. There is no other faculty that could even decipher the address. I admit that reason is a small and feeble flame, a flickering torch by stumblers carried in the starless night, — blown and flared by passion's storm, — and yet it is the only light. Extinguish that, and nought remains.

You draw a distinction between what you are pleased to call "superstition" and religion. You are shocked at the Hindoo mother when she gives her child to death at the supposed command of her God. What do you think of Abraham, of Jephthah? What is your opinion of Jehovah himself? Is not the sacrifice of a child to a phantom as horrible in Palestine as in India? Why should a God demand a sacrifice from man? Why should the infinite ask anything from the finite? Should the sun beg of the glow-worm, and should the momentary spark excite the envy of the source of light?

You must remember that the Hindoo mother believes that her child will be forever blest — that it will become the especial care of the God to whom it has been given. This is a sacrifice through a false belief on the part of the mother. She breaks her heart for the love of her babe. But what do you think of the Christian mother who expects to be happy in heaven, with her child a convict in the eternal prison — a prison in which none die, and from which none escape? What do you say of those Christians who believe that they, in heaven, will be so filled with ecstasy that all the loved of earth will be forgotten — that all the sacred relations of life, and all the passions of the heart, will fade and die, so that they will look with stony, unreplying, happy eyes upon the miseries of the lost?

You have laid down a rule by which superstition can be distinguished from religion. It is this: "It makes that a crime which is not a crime, and that a virtue which is not a virtue." Let us test your religion by this rule.

Is it a crime to investigate, to think, to reason, to observe? Is it a crime to be governed by that which to you is evidence, and is it infamous to express your honest thought? There is also another question: Is credulity a virtue? Is the open mouth of ignorant wonder the only entrance to Paradise?

According to your creed, those who believe are to be saved, and those who do not believe are to be eternally lost. When you condemn men to everlasting pain for unbelief — that is to say, for acting in accordance with that which is evidence to them — do you not make that a crime which is not a crime? And when you reward men with an eternity of joy for simply believing that which happens to be in accord with their minds, do you not make that a virtue which is not a virtue? In other words, do you not bring your own religion exactly within your own definition of superstition?

The truth is, that no one can justly be held responsible for his thoughts. The brain thinks without asking our consent. We believe, or we disbelieve, without an effort of the will. Belief is a result. It is the effect of evidence upon the mind. The scales turn in spite of him who watches. There is no opportunity of being honest or dishonest in the formation of an opinion. The conclusion is entirely independent of desire. We must believe, or we must doubt, in spite of what we wish.

That which must be, has the right to be.

We think in spite of ourselves. The brain thinks as the heart beats, as the eyes see, as the blood pursues its course in the old accustomed ways.

The question then is, not have we the right to think, — that being a necessity, — but have we the right to express our honest thoughts? You certainly have the right to express yours, and you have exercised that right. Some of your brethren, who regard me as a monster, have expressed theirs. The question now is, have I the right to express mine? In other words, have I the right to answer your letter? To make that a crime in me which is a virtue in you, certainly comes within your definition of superstition. To exercise a right yourself which you deny to me is simply the act of a tyrant. Where did you get your right to express your honest thoughts? When, and where, and how did I lose mine?

You would not burn, you would not even imprison me, because I differ with you on a subject about which neither of us knows anything. To you the savagery of the Inquisition is only a proof of the depravity of man. You are far better than your creed. You believe that even the Christian world is outgrowing the frightful feeling that fagot, and dungeon, and thumb-screw are legitimate arguments, calculated to convince those upon whom they are used, that the religion of those who use them was founded by a God of infinite compassion. You will admit that he who now persecutes for opinion's sake is infamous. And yet, the God you worship will, according to your creed, torture through all the endless years the man who entertains an honest doubt. A belief in such a God is the foundation and cause of all religious persecution. You may reply that only the belief in a false God causes believers to be inhuman. But you must admit that the Jews believed in the true God, and you are forced to say that they were so malicious, so cruel, so savage, that they crucified the only Sinless Being who ever lived. This crime was committed, not in spite of their religion, but in accordance with it. They simply obeyed the command of Jehovah. And the followers of this Sinless Being, who, for all these centuries, have denounced the cruelty of the Jews for crucifying a man on account of his opinion, have destroyed millions and millions of their fellow men for differing with them. And this same Sinless Being threatens to torture in eternal fire countless myriads for the same offence. Beyond this, inconsistency cannot go. At this point absurdity becomes infinite.

Your creed transfers the Inquisition to another world, making it eternal. Your God becomes, or rather is, an infinite Torquemada, who denies to his countless victims even the mercy of death. And this you call "a consolation."

You insist that at the foundation of every religion is the idea of God. According to your creed, all ideas of God, except those entertained by those of your faith, are absolutely false. You are not called upon to defend the Gods of the nations dead, nor the Gods of heretics. It is your business to defend the God of the Bible — the God of the Presbyterian Church. When in the ranks doing battle for your creed, you must wear the uniform of your church. You dare not say that it is sufficient to insure the salvation of a soul to believe in *a* god, or in *some* god. According to your creed, man must believe in *your* God. All the nations dead believed in gods, and all the worshipers of Zeus, and Jupiter, and Isis, and Osiris, and Brahma prayed and sacrificed in vain. Their petitions were not answered, and their souls were not saved. Surely you do not claim that it is sufficient to believe in any one of the heathen gods.

What right have you to occupy the position of the deists, and to put forth arguments that even Christians have answered? The deist denounced the God of the Bible because of his cruelty, and at the same time lauded the God of Nature. The Christian replied that the God of Nature was as cruel as the God of the Bible. This answer was complete.

I feel that you are entitled to the admission that none have been, that none are, too ignorant, too degraded, to believe in the supernatural; and I freely give you the advantage of this admission. Only a few — and they among the wisest, noblest, and purest of the human race — have regarded all gods as monstrous myths. Yet a belief in "the true God" does not seem to make men charitable or just. For most people, theism is the easiest solution of the universe. They are satisfied with saying that there must be a Being who created and who governs the world. But the universality of a belief does not tend to establish its truth. The belief in the existence of a malignant Devil has been as universal as the belief in a beneficent God, yet few intelligent men will say that the universality of this belief in an infinite demon even tends to prove his existence. In the world of thought, majorities count for nothing. Truth has always dwelt with the few.

Man has filled the world with impossible monsters, and he has been the sport and prey of these phantoms born of ignorance and hope and fear. To appease the wrath of these monsters, man has sacrificed his fellow-man. He has shed the blood of wife and child; he has fasted and prayed; he has suffered beyond the power of language to express, and yet he has received nothing from these gods — they have heard no supplication, they have answered no prayer.

You may reply that your God "sends his rain on the just and on the unjust," and that this fact proves that he is merciful to all alike. I answer, that your God sends his pestilence on the just and on the unjust — that his earthquakes devour and his cyclones rend and wreck the loving and the vicious, the honest and the criminal. Do not these facts prove that your God is cruel to all alike? In other words, do they not demonstrate the absolute impartiality of divine negligence?

Do you not believe that any honest man of average intelligence, having absolute control of the rain, could do vastly better than is being done? Certainly there would be no droughts or floods; the crops would not be permitted to wither and die, while rain was being wasted in the sea. Is it conceivable that a good man with power to control the winds would not prevent cyclones? Would you not rather trust a wise and honest man with the lightning?

Why should an infinitely wise and powerful God destroy the good and preserve the vile? Why should he treat all alike here, and in another world make an infinite difference? Why should your God allow his worshipers, his adorers, to be destroyed by his enemies? Why should he allow the honest, the loving, the noble, to perish at the stake? Can you answer these questions? Does it not seem to you that your God must have felt a touch of shame when the poor slave mother — one that had been robbed of her babe — knelt and with clasped hands, in a voice broken with sobs, commenced her prayer with the words "Our Father"?

It gave me pleasure to find that, notwithstanding your creed, you are philosophical enough to say that some men are incapacitated, by reason of temperament, for believing in the existence of God. Now, if a belief in God is necessary to the salvation of the soul, why should God create a soul without this capacity? Why should he create souls that he knew would be lost? You seem to think that it is necessary to be poetical, or dreamy, in order to be religious, and by inference, at least, you deny certain qualities to me that you deem necessary. Do you account for the atheism of Shelley by saying that he was not poetic, and do you quote his lines to prove the existence of the very God whose being he so passionately denied? Is it possible that Napoleon — one of the most infamous of men — had a nature so finely strung that he was sensitive to the divine influences? Are you driven to the necessity of proving the existence of one tyrant by the words of another? Personally, I have but little confidence in a religion that satisfied the heart of a man who, to gratify his ambition, filled half the world with widows and orphans. In regard to Agassiz, it is just to say that he furnished a vast amount of testimony in favor of the truth of the theories of Charles Darwin, and then denied the correctness of these theories — preferring the good opinions of Harvard for a few days to the lasting applause of the intellectual world.

I agree with you that the world is a mystery, not only, but that everything in nature is equally mysterious, and that there is no way of escape from the mystery of life and death. To me, the crystallization of the snow is as mysterious as the constellations. But when you endeavor to explain the mystery of the universe by the mystery of God, you do not even exchange mysteries — you simply make one more.

Nothing can be mysterious enough to become an explanation.

The mystery of man cannot be explained by the mystery of God. That mystery still asks for explanation. The mind is so that it cannot grasp the idea of an infinite personality. That is beyond the circumference. This being so, it is impossible that man can be convinced by any evidence of the existence of that which he cannot in any measure comprehend. Such evidence would be equally incomprehensible with the incomprehensible fact sought to be established by it, and the intellect of man can grasp neither the one nor the other.

You admit that the God of Nature — that is to say, your God — is as inflexible as nature itself. Why should man worship the inflexible?

Why does he kneel to the unchangeable? You say that your God "does not bend to human thought any more than to human will," and that "the more we study him, the more we find that he is not what we imagined him to be." So that, after all, the only thing you are really certain of in relation to your God is, that he is not what you think he is. Is it not almost absurd to insist that such a state of mind is necessary to salvation, or that it is a moral restraint, or that it is the foundation of social order?

The most religious nations have been the most immoral, the cruelest and the most unjust. Italy was far worse under the Popes than under the Caesars. Was there ever a barbarian nation more savage than the Spain of the sixteenth century? Certainly you must know that what you call religion has produced a thousand civil wars, and has severed with the sword all the natural ties that produce "the unity and married calm of States." Theology is the fruitful mother of discord; order is the child of reason. If you will candidly consider this question — if you will for a few moments forget your preconceived opinions — you will instantly see that the instinct of self-preservation holds society together. Religion itself was born of this instinct. People, being ignorant, believed that the Gods were jealous and revengeful. They peopled space with phantoms that demanded worship and delighted in sacrifice and ceremony, phantoms that could be flattered by praise and changed by prayer. These ignorant people wished to preserve themselves. They supposed that they could in this way avoid pestilence and famine, and postpone perhaps the day of death. Do you not see that self-preservation lies at the foundation of worship? Nations, like individuals, defend and protect themselves. Nations, like individuals, have fears, have ideals, and live for the accomplishment of certain ends. Men defend their property because it is of value. Industry is the enemy of theft. Men, as a rule, desire to live, and for that reason murder is a crime. Fraud is hateful to the victim. The majority of mankind work and produce the necessities, the comforts, and the luxuries of life. They wish to retain the fruits of their labor. Government is one of the instrumentalities for the preservation of what man deems of value. This is the foundation of social order, and this holds society together.

Religion has been the enemy of social order, because it directs the attention of man to another world. Religion teaches its votaries to sacrifice this world for the sake of that other. The effect is to weaken the ties that hold families and States together. Of what consequence is anything in this world compared with eternal joy?

You insist that man is not capable of self-government, and that God made the mistake of filling a world with failures — in other words, that man must be governed not by himself, but by your God, and that your God produces order, and establishes and preserves all the nations of the earth. This being so, your God is responsible for the government of this world. Does he preserve order in Russia? Is he accountable for Siberia? Did he establish the institution of slavery? Was he the founder of the Inquisition?

You answer all these questions by calling my attention to "the retributions of history." What are the retributions of history? The honest were burned at the stake; the patriotic, the generous, and the noble were allowed to die in dungeons; whole races were enslaved; millions of mothers were robbed of their babes. What were the retributions of history? They who committed these crimes wore crowns, and they who justified these infamies were adorned with the tiara.

You are mistaken when you say that Lincoln at Gettysburg said: "Just and true are thy judgments, Lord God Almighty." Something like this occurs in his last inaugural, in which he says, — speaking of his hope that the war might soon be ended, — "If it shall continue until every drop of blood drawn by the lash shall be paid by another drawn with the sword, still it must be said, 'The judgments of the Lord are true and righteous altogether.' " But admitting that you are correct in the assertion, let me ask you one question: Could one standing over the body of Lincoln, the blood slowly oozing from the madman's wound, have truthfully said: "Just and true are thy judgments, Lord God Almighty"?

Do you really believe that this world is governed by an infinitely wise and good God? Have you convinced even yourself of this? Why should God permit the triumph of injustice? Why should the loving be tortured? Why should the noblest be destroyed? Why should the world be filled with misery, with ignorance, and with want? What reason have you for believing that your God will do better in another world than he has done and is doing in this? Will he be wiser? Will he have more power? Will he be more merciful?

When I say "your God," of course I mean the God described in the Bible and the Presbyterian Confession of Faith. But again I say, that in the nature of things, there can be no evidence of the existence of an infinite being.

An infinite being must be conditionless, and for that reason there is nothing that a finite being can do that can by any posibility affect the well-being of the conditionless. This being so, man can neither owe nor discharge any debt or duty to an infinite being. The infinite cannot want, and man can do nothing for a being who wants nothing. A conditioned being can be made happy, or miserable, by changing conditions, but the conditionless is absolutely independent of cause and effect.

I do not say that a God does not exist, neither do I say that a God does exist; but I say that I do not know — that there can be no evidence to my mind of the existence of such a being, and that my mind is so that it is incapable of even thinking of an infinite personality. I know that in your creed you describe God as "without body, parts, or passions." This, to my mind, is simply a description of an infinite vacuum. I have had no experience with gods. This world is the only one with which I am acquainted, and I was surprised to find in your letter the expression that perhaps others are better acquainted with that of which I am so ignorant. Did you, by this, intend to say that you know anything of any other state of existence — that you have inhabited some other planet — that you lived before you were born, and that you recollect something of that other world, or of that other state?

Upon the question of immortality you have done me, unintentionally, a great injustice. With regard to that hope, I have never uttered "a flippant or a trivial" word. I have said a thousand times, and I say again, that the idea of immortality, that, like a sea, has ebbed and flowed in the human heart, with its countless waves of hope and fear beating against the shores and rocks of time and fate, was not born of any book, nor of any creed, nor of any religion. It was born of human affection, and it will continue to ebb and flow beneath the mists and clouds of doubt and darkness as long as love kisses the lips of death.

I have said a thousand times, and I say again, that we do not know, we cannot say, whether death is a wall or a door — the beginning, or end, of a day — the spreading of pinions to soar, or the folding forever of wings — the rise or the set of a sun, or an endless life, that brings rapture and love to every one.

The belief in immortality is far older than Christianity. Thousands of years before Christ was born billions of people had lived and died in that hope. Upon countless graves had been laid in love and tears the emblems of another life. The heaven of the New Testament was to be in this world. The dead, after they were raised, were to live here. Not one satisfactory word was said to have been uttered by Christ — nothing philosophic, nothing clear, nothing that adorns, like a bow of promise, the cloud of doubt.

According to the account in the New Testament, Christ was dead for a period of nearly three days. After his resurrection, why did not some one of his disciples ask him where he had been? Why did he not tell them what world he had visited? There was the opportunity to "bring life and immortality to light." And yet he was as silent as the grave that he had left — speechless as the stone that angels had rolled away.

How do you account for this? Was it not infinitely cruel to leave the world in darkness and in doubt, when one word would have filled all time with hope and light?

The hope of immortality is the great oak round which have climbed the poisonous vines of superstition. The vines have not supported the oak — the oak has supported the vines. As long as men live and love and die, this hope will blossom in the human heart.

All I have said upon this subject has been to express my hope and confess my lack of knowledge. Neither by word nor look have I expressed any other feeling than sympathy with those who hope to live again — for those who bend above their dead and dream of life to come. But I have denounced the selfishness and heartlessness of those who expect for themselves an eternity of joy, and for the rest of mankind predict, without a tear, a world of endless pain. Nothing can be more contemptible than such a hope — a hope that can give satisfaction only to the hyenas of the human race.

When I say that I do not know — when I deny the existence of perdition, you reply that "there is something very cruel in this treatment of the belief of my fellow-creatures."

You have had the goodness to invite me to a grave over which a mother bends and weeps for her only son. I accept your invitation. We will go together. Do not, I pray you, deal in splendid generalities. Be explicit. Remember that the son for whom the loving mother weeps was not a Christian, not a believer in the inspiration of the Bible nor in the divinity of Jesus Christ. The mother turns to you for consolation, for some star of hope in the midnight of her grief. What must you say? Do not desert the Presbyterian creed. Do not forget the threatenings of Jesus Christ. What must you say? Will you read a portion of the Presbyterian Confession of Faith? Will you read this?

> Although the light of Nature, and the works of creation and providence, do so far manifest the goodness, wisdom, and power of God as to leave man inexcusable, yet they are not sufficient to give that knowledge of God and of his will which is necessary to salvation.

Or, will you read this?

> By the decree of God, for the manifestation of his glory, some men and angels are predestined unto everlasting life and others foreordained to everlasting death. These angels and men, thus predestined and foreordained, are particularly and unchangeably designed, and their number is so certain and definite that it cannot be either increased or diminished.

Suppose the mother, lifting her tear-stained face, should say: "My son was good, generous, loving and kind. He gave his life for me. Is there no hope for him?" Would you then put this serpent in her breast?

> Men not professing the Christian religion cannot be saved in any other way whatsoever, be they never so diligent to conform their lives according to the light of Nature. We cannot by our best works merit pardon of sin. There is no sin so small but that it deserves damnation. Works done by unregenerate men, although, for the matter of that, they may be things which God commands, and of good use both to themselves and others, are sinful and cannot please God or make a man meet to receive Christ or God.

And suppose the mother should then sobbingly ask: "What has become of my son? Where is he now?" Would you still read from your Confession of Faith, or from your Catechism — this?

> The souls of the wicked are cast into hell, where they remain in torment and utter darkness, reserved to the judgment of the great day. At the last day the righteous shall come into everlasting life, but the wicked shall be cast into eternal torment and punished with everlasting destruction. The wicked shall be cast into hell, to be punished with unspeakable torment, both of body and soul, with the Devil and his angels forever.

If the poor mother still wept, still refused to be comforted, would you thrust this dagger in her heart?

> At the Day of Judgment you, being caught up to Christ in the clouds, shall be seated at his right hand and there openly acknowledged and acquitted, and you shall join with him in the damnation of your son.

If this failed to still the beatings of her aching heart, would you repeat these words which you say came from the loving soul of Christ?

> They who believe and are baptized shall be saved, and they who believe not shall be damned; and these shall go away into everlasting fire prepared for the Devil and his angels.

Would you not be compelled, according to your belief, to tell this mother that "there is but one name given under heaven and among men whereby" the souls of men can enter the gates of Paradise? Would you not be compelled to say: "Your son lived in a Christian land. The means of grace were within his reach. He died not having experienced a change of heart, and your son is forever lost. You can meet your son again only by dying in your sins; but if you will give your heart to God you can never clasp him to your breast again."

What could I say? Let me tell you:

"My dear madam, this reverend gentleman knows nothing of another world. He cannot see beyond the tomb. He has simply stated to you the superstitions of ignorance, of cruelty and fear. If there be in this universe a God, he certainly is as good as you are. Why should he have loved your son in life — loved him, according to this reverend gentleman, to that degree that he gave his life for him; and why should that love be changed to hatred the moment your son was dead?

"My dear woman, there are no punishments, there are no rewards — there are consequences; and of one thing you may rest assured, and that is, that every soul, no matter what sphere it may inhabit, will have the everlasting opportunity of doing right.

"If death ends all, and if this handful of dust over which you weep is all there is, you have this consolation: Your son is not within the power of this reverend gentleman's God — that is something. Your son does not suffer. Next to a life of joy is the dreamless sleep of death."

Does it not seem to you infinitely absurd to call orthodox Christianity "a consolation"? Here in this world, where every human being is enshrouded in cloud and mist, — where all lives are filled with mistakes, — where no one claims to be perfect, is it "a consolation" to say that "the smallest sin deserves eternal pain"? Is it possible for the ingenuity of man to extract from the doctrine of hell one drop, one ray, of "consolation"? If that doctrine be true, is not your God an infinite criminal? Why should he have created uncounted billions destined to suffer forever? Why did he not leave them unconscious dust?

Compared with this crime, any crime that man can by any possibility commit is a virtue.

Think for a moment of your God, — the keeper of an infinite penitentiary filled with immortal convicts, — your God an eternal turnkey, without the pardoning power. In the presence of this infinite horror, you complacently speak of the atonement, — a scheme that has not yet gathered within its horizon a billionth part of the human race, — an atonement with one-half the world remaining undiscovered for fifteen hundred years after it was made.

If there could be no suffering, there could be no sin. To unjustly cause suffering is the only possible crime. How can a God accept the suffering of the innocent in lieu of the punishment of the guilty?

According to your theory, this infinite being, by his mere will, makes right and wrong. This I do not admit. Right and wrong exist in the nature of things — in the relation they bear to man, and to sentient beings. You have already admitted that "Nature is inflexible, and that a violated law calls for its consequences." I insist that no God can step between an act and its natural effects. If God exists, he has nothing to do with punishment, nothing to do with reward. From certain acts flow certain consequences; these consequences increase or decrease the happiness of man; and the consequences must be borne.

A man who has fortified his life to the commonwealth may be pardoned, but a man who has violated a condition of his own well-being cannot be pardoned — there is no pardoning power. The laws of the State are made, and, being made, can be changed; but the facts of the universe cannot be changed. The relation of act to consequence cannot be altered. This is above all power, and, consequently, there is no analogy between the laws of the State and the facts in Nature. An infinite God could not change the relation between the diameter and circumference of the circle.

A man having committed a crime may be pardoned, but I deny the right of the State to punish an innocent man in the place of the pardoned — no matter how willing the innocent man may be to suffer the punishment. There is no law in Nature, no fact in Nature, by which the innocent can be justly punished to the end that the guilty may go free. Let it be understood once for all: Nature cannot pardon.

You have recognized this truth. You have asked me what is to become of one who seduces and betrays, of the criminal with the blood of his victim upon his hands? Without the slightest hesitation I answer, whoever commits a crime against another must, to the utmost of his power in this world and in another, if there be one, make full and ample restitution, and in addition must bear the natural consequences of his offence. No man can be perfectly happy, either in this world or in any other, who has by his perfidy broken a loving and confiding heart. No power can step between acts and consequences — no forgiveness, no atonement.

But, my dear friend, you have taught for many years, if you are a Presbyterian, or an evangelical Christian, that a man may seduce and betray, and that the poor victim, driven to insanity, leaping from some wharf at night where ships strain at their anchors in storm and darkness — you have taught that this poor girl may be tormented forever by a God of infinite compassion. This is not all that you have taught. You have said to the seducer, to the betrayer, to the one who would not listen to her wailing cry, — who would not even stretch forth his hand to catch her fluttering garments, — you have said to him: "Believe in the Lord Jesus Christ, and you shall be happy forever; you shall live in the realm of infinite delight, from which you can, without a shadow falling upon your face, observe the poor girl, your victim, writhing in the agonies of hell." You have taught this. For my part, I do not see how an angel in heaven meeting another angel whom he had robbed on the earth, could feel entirely blissful. I go further. Any decent angel, no matter if sitting at the right hand of God, should he see in hell one of his victims, would leave heaven itself for the purpose of wiping one tear from the cheek of the damned.

You seem to have forgotten your statement in the commencement of your letter, that your God is as inflexible as Nature — that he bends not to human thought nor to human will. You seem to have forgotten the line which you emphasized with italics: "*The effect of everything which is of the nature of a cause, is eternal.*" In the light of this sentence, where do you find a place for forgiveness — for your atonement? Where is a way to escape from the effect of a cause that is eternal? Do you not see that this sentence is a cord with which I easily tie your hands? The scientific part of your letter destroys the theological. You have put "new wine into old bottles," and the predicted result has followed. Will the angels in heaven, the redeemed of earth, lose their memory? Will not all the redeemed rascals remember their rascality? Will not all the redeemed assassins remember the faces of the dead? Will not all the seducers and betrayers remember her sighs, her tears, and the tones of her voice, and will not the conscience of the redeemed be as inexorable as the conscience of the damned?

If memory is to be forever "the warder of the brain," and if the redeemed can never forget the sins they committed, the pain and anguish they caused, then they can never be perfectly happy; and if the lost can never forget the good they did, the kind actions, the loving words, the heroic deeds; and if the memory of good deeds gives the slightest pleasure, then the lost can never be perfectly miserable. Ought not the memory of a good action to live as long as the memory of a bad one? So that the undying memory of the good, in heaven, brings undying pain, and the undying memory of those in hell brings undying pleasure. Do you not see that if men have done good and bad, the future can have neither a perfect heaven nor a perfect hell?

I believe in the manly doctrine that every human being must bear the consequences of his acts, and that no man can be justly saved or damned on account of the goodness or the wickedness of another.

If by atonement you mean the natural effect of self-sacrifice, the effects following a noble and disinterested action; if you mean that the life and death of Christ are worth their effect upon the human race, — which your letter seems to show, — then there is no question between us. If you have thrown away the old and barbarous idea that a law had been broken, that God demanded a sacrifice, and that Christ, the innocent, was offered up for us, and that he bore the wrath of God and suffered in our place, then I congratulate you with all my heart.

It seems to me impossible that life should be exceedingly joyous to any one who is acquainted with its miseries, its burdens, and its tears. I know that as darkness follows light around the globe, so misery and misfortune follow the sons of men. According to your creed, the future state will be worse than this. Here, the vicious may reform; here, the wicked may repent; here, a few gleams of sunshine may fall upon the darkest life. But in your future state, for countless billions of the human race, there will be no reform, no opportunity of doing right, and no possible gleam of sunshine can ever touch their souls. Do you not see that your future state is infinitely worse than this? You seem to mistake the glare of hell for the light of morning.

Let us throw away the dogma of eternal retribution. Let us "cling to all that can bring a ray of hope into the darkness of this life."

You have been kind enough to say that I find a subject for caricature in the doctrine of regeneration. If, by regeneration, you mean reformation, — if you mean that there comes a time in the life of a young man when he feels the touch of responsibility, and that he leaves his foolish or vicious ways, and concludes to act like an honest man, — if this is what you mean by regeneration, I am a believer. But that is not the definition of regeneration in your creed — that is not Christian regeneration. There is some mysterious, miraculous, supernatural, invisible agency, called, I believe, the Holy Ghost, that enters and changes the heart of man, and this mysterious agency is like the wind, under the control, apparently, of no one, coming and going when and whither it listeth. It is this illogical and absurd view of regeneration that I have attacked.

You ask me how it came to pass that a Hebrew peasant, born among the hills of Galilee, had a wisdom above that of Socrates or Plato, of Confucius or Buddha, and you conclude by saying, "This is the greatest of miracles — that such a being should live and die on the earth."

I can hardly admit your conclusion, because I remember that Christ said nothing in favor of the family relation. As a matter of fact, his life tended to cast discredit upon marriage. He said nothing against the institution of slavery; nothing against the tyranny of government; nothing of our treatment of animals; nothing about education, about intellectual progress; nothing of art, declared no scientific truth, and said nothing as to the rights and duties of nations.

You may reply that all this is included in "Do unto others as you would be done by;" and "Resist not evil." More than this is necessary to educate the human race. It is not enough to say to your child or to your pupil, "Do right." The great question still remains: What is right? Neither is there any wisdom in the idea of non-resistance. Force without mercy is tyranny. Mercy without force is but a waste of tears. Take from virtue the right of self-defence and vice becomes the master of the world.

Let me ask you how it came to pass that an ignorant driver of camels, a man without family, without wealth, became master of hundreds of millions of human beings? How is it that he conquered and overran more than half of the Christian world? How is it that on a thousand fields the banner of the cross went down in blood, while that of the crescent floated in triumph? How do you account for the fact that the flag of this imposter floats to-day above the sepulchre of Christ? Was this a miracle? Was Mohammed inspired? How do you account for Confucius, whose name is known wherever the sky bends? Was he inspired — this man who for many centuries stood first, and who has been acknowledged the superior of all men by hundreds and thousands of millions of his fellow-men? How do you account for Buddha, — in many respects the greatest religious teacher this world has ever known, — the broadest, the most intellectual of them all; he who was great enough, hundreds of years before Christ was born, to declare the universal brotherhood of man, great enough to say that intelligence is the only lever capable of raising mankind? How do you account for him, who has had more followers than any other? Are you willing to say that all success is divine? How do you account for Shakespeare, born of parents who could neither read nor write, held in the lap of ignorance and love, nursed at the breast of poverty — how do you account for him, by far the greatest of the human race, the wings of whose imagination still fill the horizon of human thought; Shakespeare, who was perfectly acquainted with the human heart, knew all depths of sorrow, all heights of joy, and in whose mind were the fruit of all thought, of all experience, and a prophecy of all to be; Shakespeare, the wisdom and beauty and depth of whose words increase with the intelligence and civilization of mankind? How do you account for this miracle? Do you believe that any founder of any religion could have written "Lear" or "Hamlet"? Did Greece produce a man who could by any possibility have been the author of "Troilus and Cressida"? Was there among all the countless millions of almighty Rome an intellect that could have written the tragedy of "Julius Cæsar"? Is not the play of "Antony and Cleopatra" as Egyptian as the Nile? How do you account for this man, within whose veins there seemed to be the blood of every race, and in whose brain there were the poetry and philosophy of a world?

You ask me to tell my opinion of Christ. Let me say here, once for all, that for the man Christ — for the man who, in the darkness, cried out, "My God, why hast thou forsaken me!" — for that man I have the greatest possible respect. And let me say, once for all, that the place where man has died for man is holy ground. To that great and serene peasant of Palestine I gladly pay the tribute of my admiration and my tears. He was a reformer in his day — an infidel in his time. Back of the theological mask, and in spite of the interpolations of the New Testament, I see a great and genuine man.

It is hard to see how you can consistently defend the course pursued by Christ himself. He attacked with great bitterness "the religion of others." It did not occur to him that "there was something very cruel in this treatment of the belief of his fellow creatures." He denounced the chosen people of God as a "generation of vipers." He compared them to "whited sepulchres." How can you sustain the conduct of missionaries? They go to other lands and attack the sacred beliefs of others. They tell the people of Indian and of all heathen lands, not only that their religion is a lie, not only that their gods are myths, but that the ancestors of these people — their fathers and mothers who never heard of God, of the Bible, or of Christ — are all in perdition. Is not this a cruel treatment of the belief of a fellow-creature?

A religion that is not manly and robust enough to bear attack with smiling fortitude is unworthy of a place in the heart or brain. A religion that takes refuge in sentimentality, that cries out: "Do not, I pray you, tell me any truth calculated to hurt my feelings," is fit only for asylums.

You believe that Christ was God, that he was infinite in power. While in Jerusalem he cured the sick, raised a few from the dead, and opened the eyes of the blind. Did he do these things because he loved mankind, or did he do these miracles simply to establish the fact that he was the very Christ? If he was actuated by love, is he not as powerful now as he was then? Why does he not open the eyes of the blind now? Why does he not with a touch make the leper clean? If you had the power to give sight to the blind, to cleanse the leper, and would not exercise it, what would be thought of you? What is the difference between one who can and will not cure, and one who causes disease?

Only the other day I saw a beautiful girl — a paralytic, and yet her brave and cheerful spirit shone over the wreck and ruin of her body like morning on the desert. What would I think of myself, had I the power by a word to send the blood through all her withered limbs freighted again with life, should I refuse?

Most theologians seem to imagine that the virtues have been produced by and are really the children of religion.

Religion has to do with the supernatural. It defines our duties and obligations to God. It prescribes a certain course of conduct by means of which happiness can be attained in another world. The result here is only an incident. The virtues are secular. They have nothing whatever to do with the supernatural, and are of no kindred to any religion. A man may be honest, courageous, charitable, industrious, hospitable, loving and pure, without being religious — that is to say, without any belief in the supernatural; and a man may be the exact opposite and at the same time a sincere believer in the creed of any church — that is to say, in the existence of a personal God, the inspiration of the Scriptures and in the divinity of Jesus Christ. A man who believes in the Bible may or may not be kind to his family, and a man who is kind and loving to his family may or may not believe in the Bible.

In order that you may see the effect of belief in the formation of character, it is only necessary to call your attention to the fact that your Bible shows that the devil himself is a believer in the existence of your God, in the inspiration of the Scriptures, and in the divinity of Jesus Christ. He not only believes these things, but he knows them, and yet, in spite of it all, he remains a devil still.

Few religions have been bad enough to destroy all the natural goodness in the human heart. In the deepest midnight of superstition some natural virtues, like stars, have been visible in the heavens. Man has committed every crime in the name of Christianity — or at least crimes that involved the commission of all others. Those who paid for labor with the lash, and who made blows a legal tender, were Christians. Those who engaged in the slave trade were believers in a personal God. One slave ship was called "The Jehovah." Those who pursued with hounds the fugitive led by the Northern star prayed fervently to Christ to crown their efforts with success, and the stealers of babes, just before falling asleep, commended their souls to the keeping of the Most High.

As you have mentioned the apostles, let me call your attention to an incident.

You remember the story of Ananias and Sapphira. The apostles, having nothing themselves, conceived the idea of having all things in common. Their followers who had something were to sell what little they had, and turn the proceeds over to the theological financiers. It seems that Ananias and Sapphira had a piece of land. They sold it and, after talking the matter over, not being entirely satisfied with the collaterals, concluded to keep a little — just enough to keep them from starvation if the good and pious bankers should abscond.

When Ananias brought the money, he was asked whether he had kept back a part of the price. He said that he had not. Whereupon God, the compassionate, struck him dead. As soon as the corpse was removed, the apostles sent for his wife. They did not tell her that her husband had been killed. They deliberately set a trap for her life. Not one of them was good enough or noble enough to put her on her guard; they allowed her to believe that her husband had told his story, and that she was free to corroborate what he had said. She probably felt that they were giving more than they could afford, and, with the instinct of woman, wanted to keep a little. She denied that any part of the price had been kept back. That moment the arrow of divine vengeance entered her heart.

Will you be kind enough to tell me your opinion of the apostles in the light of this story? Certainly murder is a greater crime than mendacity.

You have been good enough, in a kind of fatherly way, to give me some advice. You say that I ought to soften my colors, and that my words would be more weighty if not so strong. Do you really desire that I should add weight to my words? Do you really wish me to succeed?

If the commander of one army should send word to the general of the other that his men were firing too high, do you think the general would be misled? Can you conceive of his changing his orders by reason of the message?

I deny that "the Pilgrims crossed the sea to find freedom to worship God in the forests of the new world." They came not in the interest of freedom. It never entered their minds that other men had the same right to worship God according to the dictates of their consciences that the Pilgrims themselves had. The moment they had power, they were ready to whip and brand, to imprison and burn. They did not believe in religious freedom. They had no more idea of liberty of conscience than Jehovah.

I do not say that there is no place in the world for heroes and martyrs. On the contrary, I declare that the liberty we now have was won for us by heroes and by martyrs, and millions of these martyrs were burned, or flayed alive, or torn in pieces, or assassinated by the church of God. The heroism was shown in fighting the hordes of religious superstition.

Giordano Bruno was a martyr. He was a hero. He believed in no God, in no heaven, and in no hell, yet he perished by fire. He was offered liberty on condition that he would recant. There was no God to please, no heaven to expect, no hell to fear, and yet he died by fire, simply to preserve the unstained whiteness of his soul.

For hundreds of years every man who attacked the Church was a hero. The sword of Christianity has been wet for many centuries with the blood of the noblest. Christianity has been ready with whip and chain and fire to banish freedom from the earth.

Neither is it true that "family life withers under the cold sneer — half pity and half scorn — with which I look down on household worship."

Those who believe in the existence of God, and believe that they are indebted to this divine being for the few gleams of sunshine in this life, and who thank God for the little they have enjoyed, have my entire respect. Never have I said one word against the spirit of thankfulness. I understand the feeling of the man who gathers his family about him after the storm, or after the scourge, or after long sickness, and pours out his heart in thankfulness to the supposed God who has protected his fireside. I understand the spirit of the savage who thanks his idol of stone, or his fetich of wood. It is not the wisdom of the one or of the other that I respect, it is the goodness and thankfulness that prompt the prayer.

I believe in the family. I believe in family life, and one of my objections to Christianity is that it divides the family. Upon this subject I have said hundreds of times, and I say again, that the roof-tree is sacred, from the smallest fibre that feels the soft, cool clasp of earth, to the topmost flower that spreads its bosom to the sun, and like a spendthrift gives its perfume to the air. The home where virtue dwells with love is like a lily with a heart of fire, the fairest flower in all this world.

What did Christianity in the early centuries do for the home? What have nunneries and monasteries, and what has the glorification of celibacy done for the family? Do you not know that Christ himself offered rewards in this world and eternal happiness in another to those who would desert their wives and children and follow him? What effect has that promise had upon family life?

As a matter of fact, the family is regarded as nothing. Christianity teaches that there is but one family, the family of Christ, and that all other relations are as nothing compared with that. Christianity teaches the husband to desert the wife, the wife to desert the husband, children to desert their parents, for the miserable and selfish purpose of saving their own little, shriveled souls.

It is far better for man to love his fellow-men than to love God. It is better to love wife and children than to love Christ. It is better to serve your neighbor than to serve your God — even if God exists. The reason is palpable. You can do nothing for God. You can do something for wife and children. You can add to the sunshine of a life. You can plant flowers in the pathway of another.

It is true that I am an enemy of the orthodox Sabbath. It is true that I do not believe in giving one-seventh of our time to the service of superstition. The whole scheme of your religion can be understood by any intelligent man in one day. Why should he waste a seventh of his whole life in hearing the same thoughts repeated again and again?

Nothing is more gloomy than an orthodox Sabbath. The mechanic who has worked during the week in heat and dust, the laboring man who has barely succeeded in keeping his soul in his body, the poor woman who has been sewing for the rich, may go to the village church which you have described. They answer the chimes of the bell, and what do they hear in this village church? Is it that God is the Father of the human race; is that all? If that were all, you never would have heard an objection from my lips. That is not all. If all ministers said: Bear the evils of this life; your Father in heaven counts your tears; the time will come when pain and death and grief will be forgotten words; I should have listened with the rest. What else does the minister say to the poor people who have answered the chimes of your bell? He says:

"The smallest sin deserves eternal pain." "A vast majority of men are doomed to suffer the wrath of God forever." He fills the present with fear and the future with fire. He has heaven for the few, hell for the many. He decribes a little grass-grown path that leads to heaven, where travelers are "few and far between," and a great highway worn with countless feet that leads to everlasting death.

Such Sabbaths are immoral. Such ministers are the real savages. Gladly would I abolish such a Sabbath. Gladly would I turn it into a holiday, a day of rest and peace, a day to get acquainted with your wife and children, a day to exchange civilities with your neighbors; and gladly would I see the church in which such sermons are preached changed to a place of entertainment. Gladly would I have the echoes of orthodox sermons — the owls and bats among the rafters, the snakes in crevices and corners — driven out by the glorious music of Wagner and Beethoven. Gladly would I see the Sunday school where the doctrine of eternal fire is taught, changed to a happy dance upon the village green.

Music refines. The doctrine of eternal punishment degrades. Science civilizes. Superstition looks longingly back to savagery.

You do not believe that general morality can be upheld without the sanctions of religion.

Christianity has sold, and continues to sell, crime on a credit. It has taught, and it still teaches, that there is forgiveness for all. Of course it teaches morality. It says: "Do not steal, do not murder;" but it adds, "but if you do both, there is a way of escape: believe on the Lord Jesus Christ and thou shalt be saved." I insist that such a religion is no restraint. It is far better to teach that there is no forgiveness, and that every human being must bear the consequences of his acts.

The first great step toward national reformation is the universal acceptance of the idea that there is no escape from the consequences of our acts. The young men who come from their country homes into a city filled with temptations may be restrained by the thought of father and mother. This is a natural restraint. They may be restrained by their knowledge of the fact that a thing is evil on account of its consequences, and that to do wrong is always a mistake. I cannot conceive of such a man being more liable to temptation because he has heard one of my lectures in which I have told him that the only good is happiness — that the only way to attain that good is by doing what he believes to be right. I cannot imagine that his moral character will be weakened by the statement that there is no escape from the consequences of his acts. You seem to think that he will be instantly led astray — that he will go off under the flaring lamps to the riot of passion. Do you think the Bible calculated to restrain him? To prevent this would you recommend him to read the lives of Abraham, of Isaac, and of Jacob, and the other holy polygamists of the Old Testament? Should he read the life of David, and of Solomon? Do you think this would enable him to withstand temptation? Would it not be far better to fill the young man's mind with facts so that he may know exactly the physical consequences of such acts? Do you regard ignorance as the foundation of virtue? Is fear the arch that supports the moral nature of man?

You seem to think that there is danger in knowledge, and that the best chemists are most likely to poison themselves.

You say that to sneer at religion is only a step from sneering at morality, and then only another step to that which is vicious and profligate.

The Jews entertained the same opinion of the teaching of Christ. He sneered at their religion. The Christians have entertained the same opinion of every philosopher. Let me say to you again — and let me say it once for all — that morality has nothing to do with religion. Morality does not depend upon the supernatural. Morality does not walk with the crutches of miracles. Morality appeals to the experience of mankind. It cares nothing about faith, nothing about sacred books. Morality depends upon facts, something that can be seen, something known, the product of which can be estimated. It needs no priest, no ceremony, no mummery. It believes in the freedom of the human mind. It asks for investigation. It is founded upon truth. It is the enemy of all religion, because it has to do with this world, and with this world alone.

My object is to drive fear out of the world. Fear is the jailer of the mind. Christianity, superstition — that is to say, the supernatural — makes every brain a prison and every soul a convict. Under the government of a personal deity, consequences partake of the nature of punishments and rewards. Under the government of Nature, what you call punishments and rewards are simply consequences. Nature does not punish. Nature does not reward. Nature has no purpose. When the storm comes, I do not think: "This is being done by a tyrant." When the sun shines, I do not say: "This is being done by a friend." Liberty means freedom from personal dictation. It does not mean escape from the relations we sustain to other facts in Nature. I believe in the restraining influences of liberty. Temperance walks hand in hand with freedom. To remove a chain from the body puts an additional responsibility upon the soul. Liberty says to the man: You injure or benefit yourself; you increase or decrease your own well-being. It is a question of intelligence. You need not bow to a supposed tyrant, or to infinite goodness. You are responsible to yourself and to those you injure, and to none other.

I rid myself of fear, believing as I do that there is no power above which can help me in any extremity, and believing as I do that there is no power above or below that can injure me in any extremity. I do not believe that I am the sport of accident, or that I may be dashed in pieces by the blind agency of Nature. There is no accident, and there is no agency. That which happens must happen. The present is the necessary child of all the past, the mother of all the future.

Does it relieve mankind from fear to believe that there is some God who will help them in extremity? What evidence have they on which to found this belief? When has any God listened to the prayer of any man? The water drowns, the cold freezes, the flood destroys, the fire burns, the bolt of heaven falls — when and where has the prayer of man been answered?

Is the religious world today willing to test the efficacy of prayer? Only a few years ago it was tested in the United States. The Christians of Christendom, with one accord, fell upon their knees and asked God to spare the life of one man. You know the result. You know just as well as I that the forces of Nature produce the good and bad alike. You know that the forces of Nature destroy the good and bad alike. You know that the lightning feels the same keen delight in striking to death the honest man that it does or would in striking the assassin with his knife lifted above the bosom of innocence.

Did God hear the prayers of the slaves? Did he hear the prayers of imprisoned philosophers and patriots? Did he hear the prayers of martyrs, or did he allow fiends, calling themselves his followers, to pile the fagots round the forms of glorious men? Did he allow the flames to devour the flesh of those whose hearts were his? Why should any man depend on the goodness of a God who created countless millions, knowing that they would suffer eternal grief?

The faith that you call sacred — "sacred as the most delicate manly or womanly sentiment of love and honor" — is the faith that nearly all of your fellow-men are to be lost. Ought an honest man to be restrained from denouncing that faith because those who entertain it say that their feelings are hurt? You say to me: "There is a hell. A man advocating the opinions you advocate will go there when he dies." I answer: "There is no hell. The Bible that teaches it is not true." And you say: "How can you hurt my feelings?"

You seem to think that one who attacks the religion of his parents is wanting in respect to his father and his mother.

Were the early Christians lacking in respect for their fathers and mothers? Were the Pagans who embraced Christianity heartless sons and daughters? What have you to say of the apostles? Did they not heap contempt upon the religion of their fathers and mothers? Did they not join with him who denounced their people as a "generation of vipers"? Did they not follow one who offered a reward to those who would desert fathers and mothers? Of course you have only to go back a few generations in your family to find a Field who was not a Presbyterian. After that you find a Presbyterian. Was he base enough and infamous enough to heap contempt upon the religion of his father and mother? All the Protestants in the time of Luther lacked in respect for the religion of their fathers and mothers. According to your idea, Progress is a Prodigal Son. If one is bound by the religion of his father and mother, and his father happens to be a Presbyterian and his mother a Catholic, what is he to do? Do you not see that your doctrine gives intellectual freedom only to foundlings?

If by Christianity you mean the goodness, the spirit of forgiveness, the benevolence claimed by Christians to be a part, and the principal part, of that peculiar religion, then I do not agree with you when you say that "Christ is Christianity and that it stands or falls with him." You have narrowed unnecessarily the foundation of your religion. If it should be established beyond doubt that Christ never existed, all that is of value in Christianity would remain, and remain unimpaired. Suppose that we should find that Euclid was a myth, the science known as mathematics would not suffer. It makes no difference who painted or chiseled the greatest pictures and statues, so long as we have the pictures and statues. When he who has given the world a truth passes from the earth, the truth is left. A truth dies only when forgotten by the human race. Justice, love, mercy, forgiveness, honor, all the virtues that ever blossomed in the human heart, were known and practiced for uncounted ages before the birth of Christ.

You insist that religion does not leave man in "abject terror" — does not leave him "in utter darkness as to his fate."

Is it possible to know who will be saved? Can you read the names mentioned in the decrees of the Infinite? Is it possible to tell who is to be eternally lost? Can the imagination conceive a worse fate than your religion predicts for a majority of the race? Why should not every human being be in "abject terror" who believes your doctrine? How many loving and sincere women are in the asylums to-day fearing that they have committed "the unpardonable sin" — a sin to which your

God has attached the penalty of eternal torment, and yet has failed to describe the offence? Can tyranny go beyond this — fixing the penalty of eternal pain for the violation of a law not written, not known, but kept in the secrecy of infinite darkness? How much happier it is to know nothing about it, and to believe nothing about it! How much better to have no God!

You discover a "Great Intelligence ordering our little lives, so that even the trials that we bear, as they call out the finer elements of character, conduce to our future happiness." This is an old explanation — probably as good as any. The idea is, that this world is a school in which man becomes educated through tribulation — the muscles of character being developed by wrestling with misfortune. If it is necessary to live this life in order to develop character, in order to become worthy of a better world, how do you account for the fact that billions of the human race die in infancy, and are thus deprived of this necessary education and development? What would you think of a schoolmaster who should kill a large proportion of his scholars during the first day, before they had even had the opportunity to look at A?

You insist that "there is a power behind Nature making for righteousness."

If Nature is infinite, how can there be a power outside of Nature? If you mean by "a power making for righteousness" that man, as he becomes civilized, as he becomes intelligent, not only takes advantage of the forces of Nature for his own benefit, but perceives more and more clearly that if he is to be happy he must live in harmony with the conditions of his being, in harmony with the facts by which he is surrounded, in harmony with the relations he sustains to others and to things; if this is what you mean, then there is "a power making for righteousness." But if you mean that there is something supernatural back of Nature directing events, then I insist that there can by no possibility be any evidence of the existence of such a power.

The history of the human race shows that nations rise and fall. There is a limit to the life of a race; so that it can be said of every dead nation, that there was a period when it laid the foundations of prosperity, when the combined intelligence and virtue of the people constituted a power working for righteousness, and that there came a time when this nation became a spendthrift, when it ceased to accumulate te, when it lived on the labors of its youth, and passed rom strength and glory to the weakness of old age, and finally fell palsied to its tomb.

The intelligence of man guided by a sense of duty is the only power that makes for righteousness.

You tell me that I am waging "a hopeless war," and you give as a reason that the Christian religion began to be nearly two thousand years before I was born, and that it will live two thousand years after I am dead.

Is this an argument? Does it tend to convince even yourself? Could not Caiaphas, the high priest, have said substantially this to Christ? Could he not have said: "The religion of Jehovah began to be four thousand years before you were born, and it will live two thousand years after you are dead"? Could not a follower of Buddha make the same illogical remark to a missionary from Andover with the glad tidings? Could he not say: "You are waging a hopeless war. The religion of Buddha began to be twenty-five hundred years before you were born, and hundreds of millions of people still worship at Great Buddha's shrine"?

Do you insist that nothing except the right can live for two thousand years? Why is it that the Catholic Church "lives on and on, while nations and kingdoms perish"? Do you consider that the "survival of the fittest"?

Is it the same Christian religion now living that lived during the Middle Ages? Is it the same Christian religion that founded the Inquisition and invented the thumbscrew? Do you see no difference between the religion of Calvin and Jonathan Edwards and the Christianity of today? Do you really think that it is the same Christianity that has been living all these years? Have you noticed any change in the last generation? Do you remember when scientists endeavored to prove a theory by a passage from the Bible, and do you now know that believers in the Bible are exceedingly anxious to prove its truth by some fact that science has demonstrated? Do you know that the standard has changed? Other things are not measured by the Bible, but the Bible has to submit to another test. It no longer owns the scales. It has to be weighed, — it is being weighed, — it is growing lighter and lighter every day. Do you know that only a few years ago "the glad tidings of great joy" consisted mostly in a description of hell? Do you know that nearly every intelligent minister is now ashamed to preach about it, or to read about it, or to talk about it? Is there any change? Do you know that few ministers now believe in the "plenary inspiration" of the Bible, that from thousands of pulpits people are now told that the creation according to Genesis is a mistake, that it never was as wet as the flood, and that the miracles of the Old Testament are considered simply as myths or mistakes?

How long will what you call Christianity endure, if it changes as rapidly during the next century as it has during the last? What will there be left of the supernatural?

It does not seem possible that thoughtful people can, for many years, believe that a being of infinite wisdom is the author of the Old Testament, that a being of infinite purity and kindness upheld polygamy and slavery, that he ordered his chosen people to massacre their neighbors, and that he commanded husbands and fathers to persecute wives and daughters unto death for opinion's sake.

It does not seem within the prospect of belief that Jehovah, the cruel, the jealous, the ignorant, and the revengeful, is the creator and preserver of the universe.

Does it seem possible that infinite goodness would create a world in which life feeds on life, in which everything devours and is devoured? Can there be a sadder fact than this: Innocence is not a certain shield?

It is impossible for me to believe in the eternity of punishment. If that doctrine be true, Jehovah is insane.

Day after day there are mournful processions of men and women, patriots and mothers, girls whose only crime is that the word Liberty burst into flower between their pure and loving lips, driven like beasts across the melancholy wastes of Siberian snow. These men, these women, these daughters, go to exile and to slavery, to a land where hope is satisfied with death. Does it seem possible to you that an "Infinite Father" sees all this and sits as silent as a god of stone?

And yet, according to your Presbyterian creed, according to your inspired book, according to your Christ, there is another procession, in which are the noblest and the best, in which you will find the wondrous spirits of this world, the lovers of the human race, the teachers of their fellow-men, the greatest soldiers that ever battled for the right; and this procession of countless millions, in which you will find the most generous and the most loving of the sons and daughters of men, is moving on to the Siberia of God, the land of eternal exile, where agony becomes immortal.

How can you, how can any man with brain or heart, believe this infinite lie?

Is there not room for a better, for a higher philosophy? After all, is it not possible that we may find that everything has been necessarily produced, that all religions and superstitions, all mistakes and all crimes, were simply necessities? Is it not possible that out of this perception may come not only love and pity for others, but absolute justification for the individual? May we not find that every soul has, like Mazeppa, been lashed to the wild horse of passion, or like Prometheus to the rocks of fate?

You ask me to take the "sober second thought." I beg of you to take the first, and if you do, you will throw away the Presbyterian creed; you will instantly perceive that he who commits the "smallest sin" no more deserves eternal pain than he who does the smallest virtuous deed deserves eternal bliss; you will become convinced that an infinite God who creates billions of men knowing that they will suffer through all the countless years is an infinite demon; you will be satisfied that the Bible, with its philosophy and its folly, with its goodness and its cruelty, is but the work of man, and that the supernatural does not and cannot exist.

For you personally, I have the highest regard and the sincerest respect, and I beg of you not to pollute the soul of childhood, not to furrow the cheeks of mothers, by preaching a creed that should be shrieked in a mad-house. Do not make the cradle as terrible as the coffin. Preach, I pray you, the gospel of Intellectual Hospitality — the liberty of thought and speech. Take from loving hearts the awful fear. Have mercy on your fellow-men. Do not drive to madness the mothers whose tears are falling on the pallid faces of those who died in unbelief. Pity the erring, wayward, suffering, weeping world. Do not proclaim as "tidings of great joy" that an Infinite Spider is weaving webs to catch the souls of men.

Robert G. Ingersoll

A Last Word to Robert G. Ingersoll

My Dear Colonel Ingersoll:

I have read your Reply to my Open Letter half a dozen times, and each time with new appreciation of your skill as an advocate. It is written with great ingenuity, and furnishes probably as complete an argument as you are able to give for the faith (or want of faith) that is in you. Doubtless you think it unanswerable, and so it will seem to those who are predisposed to your way of thinking. To quote a homely saying of Mr. Lincoln, in which there is as much of wisdom as of wit, "For those who like that sort of thing, no doubt that is the sort of thing they do like." You may answer that we, who cling to the faith of our fathers, are equally prejudiced, and that it is for that reason that we are not more impressed by the force of your pleading. I do not deny a strong leaning that way, and yet our real interest is the same — to get at the truth; and, therefore, I have tried to give due weight to whatever of argument there is in the midst of so much eloquence; but must confess that, in spite of all, I remain in the same obdurate frame of mind as before. With all the candor that I can bring to bear upon the question, I find on reviewing my Open Letter scarcely a sentence to change and nothing to withdraw; and am quite willing to leave it as my Declaration of Faith, to stand side by side with your Reply, for intelligent and candid men to judge between us. I need only to add a few words in taking leave of the subject.

You seem a little disturbed that "some of my brethren" should look upon you as "a monster" because of your unbelief. I certainly do not approve of such language, although they would tell me that it is the only word which is a fit response to your ferocious attacks upon what they hold most sacred. You are a born gladiator, and when you descend into the arena, you strike heavy blows, which provoke blows in return. In this very Reply you manifest a particular animosity against Presbyterians. Is it because you were brought up in that Church, of which your father, whom you regard with filial respect and affection, was an honored minister? You even speak of "the Presbyterian God!" as if we assumed to appropriate the Supreme Being, claiming to be the special objects of His favor. Is there any ground for this imputation of narrowness? On the contrary, when we bow our knees before our Maker, it is as the God and Father of all mankind; and the expression you permit yourself to use, can only be regarded as grossly offensive. Was it necessary to offer this rudeness to the religious denomination in which you were born?

And this may explain, what you do not seem fully to understand, why it is that you are sometimes treated to sharp epithets by the religious press and public. You think yourself persecuted for your opinions. But others hold the same opinions without offence. Nor is it because you express your opinions. Nobody would deny you the same freedom which is accorded to Huxley or Herbert Spencer. It is not because you exercise your liberty of judgment or of speech, but because of the way in which you attack others, holding up their faith to all manner of ridicule, and speaking of those who profess it as if they must be either knaves or fools. It is not in human nature not to resent such imputations on that which, however incredible to you, is very precious to them. Hence it is that they think you a rough antagonist; and when you shock them by such expressions as I have quoted, you must expect some pretty strong language in return. I do not join them in this, because I know you, and appreciate that other side of you which is manly and kindly and chivalrous. But while I recognize these better qualities, I must add in all frankness that I am compelled to look upon you as a man so embittered against religion that you cannot think of it except as associated with cant, bigotry, and hypocrisy. In such a state of mind it is hardly possible for you to judge fairly of the arguments for its truth.

I believe with you, that reason was given us to be exercised, and that when man seeks after truth, his mind should be, as you say Darwin's was, "as free from prejudice as the mariner's compass." But if he is warped by passion so that he cannot see things truly, then is he responsible. It is the moral element which alone makes the responsibility. Nor do I believe that any man will be judged in this world or the next for what does not involve a moral wrong. Hence your appalling statement, "The God you worship will, according to your creed, torture (!) through all the endless years the man who entertains an honest doubt" does not produce the effect intended, simply because I do not affirm nor believe any such thing. I believe that, in the future world, every man will be judged according to the deeds done in the body, and that the judgment, whatever it may be, will be transparently just. God is more merciful than man. He desireth not the death of the wicked. Christ forgave, where men would condemn, and whatever be the fate of any human soul, it can never be said that the Supreme Ruler was wanting either in justice or mercy. This I emphasize because you dwell so much upon the subject of future retribution, giving it an attention so constant as to be almost exclusive. Whatever else you touch upon, you soon come back to this as the black thundercloud that darkens all the horizon, casting its mighty shadows over the life that now is and that which is to come. Your denunciations of this "inhuman" belief are so reiterated that one would be left to infer that there is nothing else in Religion, that it is all wrath and terror. But this is putting a part for the whole. Religion is a vast system, of which this is but a single feature: It is but one doctrine of many; and indeed some whom no one will deny to be devout Christians, do not hold it at all, or only in a modified form, while with all their hearts they accept and profess the Religion that Christ came to bring into the world.

Archdeacon Farrar, of Westminster Abbey, the most eloquent preacher in the Church of England, has written a book entitled "Eternal Hope," in which he argues from reason and the Bible, that this life is not "the be-all and end-all" of human probation; but that in the world to come there will be another opportunity, when countless millions, made wiser by unhappy experience, will turn again to the paths of life; and that so in the end the whole human race, with the exception of perhaps a few who remain irreclaimable, will be recovered and made happy forever. Others look upon "eternal death" as merely the extinction of being, while immortality is the reward of pre-eminent virtue, interpreting in that sense the words, "The wages of sin is death but the gift of God is eternal life through Jesus Christ our Lord." The latter view might recommend itself to you as the application of "the survival of the fittest" to another world, the worthless, the incurably bad, of the human race being allowed to drop out of existence (an end which can have no terrors for you, since you look upon it as the common lot of all men), while the good are continued in being forever. The acceptance of either of these theories would relieve your mind of that "horror of great darkness" which seems to come over it whenever you look forward to retribution beyond the grave.

But while conceding all liberty to others I cannot so easily relieve myself of this stern and rugged truth. To me moral evil in the universe is a tremendous reality, and I do not see how to limit it within the bounds of time. Retribution is to me a necessary part of the Divine law. A law without a penalty for its violations is no law. But I rest the argument for it, not on the Bible, but *on principles which you yourself acknowledge*. You say, "There are no punishments, no rewards: there are consequences." Very well, take the "consequences," and see where they lead you. When a man by his vices has reduced his body to a wreck and his mind to idiocy, you say this is the "consequence" of his vicious life. Is it a great stretch of language to say that it is his "punishment," and none the less punishment because self-inflicted? To the poor sufferer raving in a madhouse, it matters little what it is called, so long as he is experiencing the agonies of hell. And here your theory of "consequences," if followed up, will lead you very far. For if man lives after death, and keeps his personal identity, do not the "consequences" of his past life follow him into the future? And if his existence is immortal, are not the consequences immortal also? And what is this but endless retribution?

But you tell me that the moral effect of retribution is detroyed by the easy way in which a man escapes the penalty. He has but to repent, and he is restored to the same condition before the law as if he had not sinned. Not so do I understand it. "I believe in the forgiveness of sins," but forgiveness does not reverse the course of nature; it does not prevent the operation of natural law. A drunkard may repent as he is nearing his end, but that does not undo the wrong that he has done, nor avert the consequences. In spite of his tears, he dies in an agony of shame and remorse. The inexorable law must be fulfilled.

And so in the future world. Even though a man be forgiven, he does not wholly escape the evil of his past life. A retribution follows him even within the heavenly gates; for if he does not *suffer*, still that bad life has so shriveled up his moral nature as to diminish his power of enjoyment. There are degrees of happiness, as one star differeth from another star in glory; and he, who begins wrong, will find that it is not as well to sin and repent of it as not to sin at all. He enters the other world in a state of spiritual infancy and will have to begin at the bottom and climb slowly upward.

We might go a step farther and say that perhaps heaven itself has not only its lights but its shadows, in the reflections that must come even there. We read of "the book of God's remembrance," but is there not another book of remembrance in the mind itself — a book which any man may well fear to open and to look thereon? When that book is opened, and we read its awful pages, shall we not all think "what might have been?" And will those thoughts be wholly free from sadness? The drunken brute who breaks the heart that loved him may weep bitterly, and his poor wife may forgive him with her dying lips, but *he cannot forgive himself*, and *never* can he recall without grief that bowed head and that broken heart. This preserves the element of retribution, while it does not shut the door to forgiveness and mercy.

But we need not travel over again the round of Christian doctrines. My faith is very simple; it revolves around two words — GOD and CHRIST. These are the two centres, or, as an astronomer might say, the double-star, or double-sun, of the great orbit of religious truth.

As to the first of these, you say "There can be no evidence to my mind of the existence of such a being, and my mind is so that it is incapable of even thinking of an infinite personality;" and you gravely put to me this question: "Do you really believe that this world is governed by an infinitely wise and good God? Have you convinced even yourself of this?" Here are two questions — one as to the existence of God, and the other as to His benevolence. I will answer both in language as plain as it is possible for me to use.

First, Do I believe in the existence of God? I answer that it is impossible for me *not* to believe it. I could not disbelieve it if I would. You insist that belief or unbelief is not a matter of choice or of the will, but of evidence. You say "the brain thinks as the heart beats, as the eyes see." Then let us stand aside with all our prepossessions and open our eyes to what we can see.

When Robinson Crusoe in his desert island came down one day to the seashore, and saw in the sand the print of a human foot, could he help the instantaneous conviction that a man had been there? You might have tried to persuade him that it was all chance, — that the sand had been washed up by the waves or blown by the winds, and taken this form, or that some marine insect had traced a figure like a human foot, — you would not have moved him a particle. The imprint was there, and the conclusion was irresistible: he did not believe — he *knew* that some human being, whether friend or foe, civilized or savage, had set his foot upon that desolate shore. So when I discover in the world (as I think I do) mysterious footprints that are certainly not human, it is not a question whether I shall believe or not: I cannot help believing that some Power greater than man has set foot upon the earth.

It is a fashion among atheistic philosophers to make light of the argument from design; but "my mind is so that it is incapable" of resisting the conclusion to which it leads me. And (since personal questions are in order) I beg to ask if it is possible for *you* to take in your hands a watch, and believe that there was no "design" in its construction; that it was not made to keep time, but only "happened" so; that it is the product of some freak of nature, which brought together its parts and set it going. Do you not *know* with as much positiveness as can belong to any conviction of your mind, that it was *not* the work of accident, but of design; and that if there was a design, there was a designer? And if the watch was made to keep time, was not the eye made to see and the ear to hear? Skeptics may fight against this argument as much as they please, and try to evade the inevitable conclusion, and yet it remains forever entwined in the living frame of man as well as imbedded in the solid foundations of the globe. Wherefore I repeat, it is not a question with me whether I *will* believe or not — I cannot help believing; and I am not only surprised, but amazed, that you or any thoughtful man can come to any other conclusion. In wonder and astonishment I ask, "Do you really believe" that in all the wide universe there is no Higher Intelligence than that of the poor human creatures that creep on this earthly ball? For myself, it is with the profoundest conviction as well as the deepest reverence that I repeat the first sentence of my faith: "I believe in God the Father Almighty."

And not the Almighty only, but the Wise and the Good. Again I ask, How can I help believing what I see every day of my life? Every morning, as the sun rises in the East, sending light and life over the world, I behold a glorious image of the beneficent Creator. The exquisite beauty of the dawn, the dewy freshness of the air, the fleecy clouds floating in the sky — all speak of Him. And when the sun goes down, sending shafts of light through the dense masses that would hide his setting, and casting a glory over the earth and sky, this wondrous illumination is to me but the reflection of Him who "spreadeth out the heavens like a curtain; who maketh the clouds His chariot; who walketh upon the wings of the wind."

How much more do we find the evidences of goodness in man himself: in the power of thought; of acquiring knowledge; of penetrating the mysteries of nature and climbing among the stars. Can a being endowed with such transcendent gifts doubt the goodness of his Creator?

Yes, I believe with all my heart and soul in One who is not only

Infinitely Great, but Infinitely Good, who loves all the creatures He has made, bending over them as the bow in the cloud spans the arch of heaven, stretching from horizon to horizon; looking down upon them with a tenderness compared to which all human love is faint and cold. "Like as a father pitieth his children, so the Lord pitieth them that fear Him; for He knoweth our frame, He remembereth that we are dust."

On the question of immortality you are equally "at sea." You know nothing and believe nothing; or, rather, you know only that you do *not* know, and believe that you do *not* believe. You confess indeed to a faint hope, and admit a bare possibility, that there may be another life, though you are in an uncertainty about it that is altogether bewildering and desperate. But your mind is so poetical that you give a certain attractiveness even to the prospect of annihilation. You strew the sepulchre with such flowers as these:

> I have said a thousand times, and I say again, that the idea of immortality, that like a sea has ebbed and flowed in the human heart, with its countless waves of hope and fear beating against the shores and rocks of time and fate, was not born of any book, nor of any creed, nor of any religion. It was born of human affection, and it will continue to ebb and flow beneath the mists and clouds of doubt and darkness as long as love kisses the lips of death.
>
> I have said a thousand times, and I say again, that we do not know, we cannot say, whether death is a wall or a door; the beginning or end of a day; the spreading of pinions to soar, or the folding forever of wings; the rise or the set of a sun, or an endless life that brings rapture and love to every one.

Beautiful words! but inexpressibly sad! It is a silver lining to the cloud, and yet the cloud is there, dark and impenetrable. But perhaps we ought not to expect anything clearer and brighter from one who recognizes no light but that of Nature. That light is very dim. If it were all we had, we should be just where Cicero was and say with him, and with you, that a future life was "to be hoped for rather than believed." But does not that very uncertainty show the need of a something above Nature, which is furnished in Him who "was crucified, dead and buried, and the third day rose again from the dead?" It is the Conquerer of Death who calls to the fainthearted: "I am the Resurrection and the Life." Since He has gone before us, lighting up the dark passage of the grave, we need not fear to follow, resting on the word of our Leader:

"Because I live, ye shall live also."

This faith in another life is a precious inheritance, which cannot be torn from the agonized bosom without a wrench that tears every heartstring; and it was to this I referred as the last refuge of a poor, suffering, despairing soul, when I asked: "Does it never occur to you that there is something very cruel in this treatment of the belief of your fellow-creatures, on whose hope of another life hangs all that relieves the darkness of their present existence?" The imputation of cruelty you repel with some warmth, saying (with a slight variation of my language): *"When I deny the existence of perdition,* you reply that there is something very cruel in this treatment of the belief of my fellow-creatures." Of course, this change of words, putting *perdition* in the place of immortal life and hope, was a mere inadvertence. But it was enough to change the whole character of what I wrote. As I described "the treatment of the belief of my fellow-creatures," I did think it "very cruel," and I think so still.

While correcting this slight misquotation, I must remove from your mind a misapprehension, which is so very absurd as to be absolutely comical. In my Letter referring to your disbelief of immortality, I had said: "With an air of modesty and diffidence that would carry an audience by storm, you confess your ignorance of what perhaps others are better acquainted with, when you say, 'This world is all that *I* know anything about, *so far as I recollect.*' " Of course "what perhaps others are better acquainted with" was a part of what you said, or at least implied by your manner (for you do not convey your meaning merely by words, but by a tone of voice, by arched eyebrows, or a curled lip), and yet, instead of taking the sentence in its plain and obvious sense, you affect to understand it as an assumption on my part to have some private and mysterious knowledge of another world (!), and gravely ask me, "Did you by this intend to say that you know anything of any other state of existence; that you have inhabited some other planet; that you lived before you were born; and that you recollect something of that other world or of that other state?" No, my dear Colonel! I have been a good deal of a traveler, and have seen all parts of this world, but I have never visited any other. In reading your sober question, if I did not know you to be one of the brightest wits of the day, I should be tempted to quote what Sidney Smith says of a Scotchman, that "you cannot get a joke into his head except by a surgical operation!"

But to return to what is serious: you make light of our faith and our hopes, because you know not the infinite solace they bring to the troubled human heart. You sneer at the idea that religion can be a "consolation." Indeed! Is it not a consolation to have an Almighty Friend? Was it a light matter for the poor slave mother, who sat alone in her cabin, having been robbed of her children, to sing in her wild, wailing accents: "Nobody knows the sorrows I've seen: Nobody knows but Jesus"? Would you rob her of that Unseen Friend — the only Friend she had on earth or in heaven?

But I will do you the justice to say that your want of religious faith comes in part from your very sensibility and tenderness of heart. You cannot recognize an overruling Providence, because your mind is so harassed by scenes that you witness. Why, you ask, do men suffer so? You draw frightful pictures of the misery which exists in the world, as a proof of the incapacity of its Ruler and Governor, and do not hesitate to say that "any honest man of average intelligence could do vastly better." If you could have your way, you would make everybody happy; there should be no more poverty, and no more sickness or pain.

This is a pleasant picture to look at, and yet you must excuse me for saying that it is rather a child's picture than that of a stalwart man. The world is not a playground in which men are to be petted and indulged like children: spoiled children they would soon become. It is an arena of conflict, in which we are to develop the manhood that is in us. We all have to take the "rough-and-tumble" of life, and are the better for it — physically, intellectually, and morally. If there be any true manliness within us, we come out of the struggle stronger and better; with larger minds and kinder hearts; a broader wisdom and a gentler charity.

Perhaps we should not differ on this point if we could agree as to the true end of life. But here I fear the difference is irreconcilable. You think that end is happiness: I think it is CHARACTER. I do not believe that the highest end of life upon earth is to "have a good time;" to get from it the utmost amount of enjoyment; but to be truly and greatly GOOD; and that to that end no discipline can be too severe which leads us "to suffer and be strong." That discipline answers its end when it raises the spirit to the highest pitch of courage and endurance. The splendor of virtue never appears so bright as when set against a dark background. It was in prisons and dungeons that the martyrs showed the greatest degree of moral heroism, the power of "Man's unconquerable mind."

But I know well that these illustrations do not cover the whole case. There is another picture to be added to those of heroic struggle and martyrdom — that of silent suffering, which makes of life one long agony, and which often comes upon the good, so that it seems as if the best suffered the most. And yet when you sit by a sick bed, and look into a face whiter than the pillow on which it rests, do you not sometimes mark how that very suffering refines the nature that bears it so meekly? This is the Christian theory: that suffering, patiently borne, is a means of the greatest elevation of character and, in the end, of the highest enjoyment. Looking at it in this light, we can understand how it should be that "the sufferings of this present time are not worthy to be compared [or even to be named] with the glory which shall be revealed." When the heavenly morning breaks, brighter than any dawn that blushes "o'er the world," there will be "a restitution of all things:" the poor will be made rich, and the most suffering the most serenely happy; as in the vision of the Apocalypse, when it is asked "What are these which are arrayed in white robes, and whence came they?" the answer is, "These are they which came out of great tribulation."

In this conclusion, which is not adopted lightly, but after innumerable struggles with doubt, after the experience and the reflection of years, I feel "a great peace." It is the glow of sunset that gilds the approach of evening. For (we must confess it) it is towards that you and I are advancing. The sun has passed the meridian, and hastens to his going down. Whatever of good this life has for us (and I am far from being one of those who look upon it as a vale of tears) will soon be behind us. I see the shadows creeping on; yet I welcome the twilight that will soon darken into night, for I know that it will be a night all glorious with stars. As I look upward, the feeling of awe is blended with a strange, overpowering sense of the Infinite Goodness, which surrounds me like an atmosphere:

And so beside the Silent Sea,
I wait the muffled oar;
No harm from Him can come to me
On ocean or on shore.

I know not where His Islands lift
Their fronded palms in air;
I only know I cannot drift
Beyond His love and care.

Would that you could share with me this confidence and this hope! But you seem to be receding farther from any kind of faith. In one of your closing paragraphs, you give what is to you "the conclusion of the matter." After repudiating religion with scorn, you ask, "Is there not room for a better, for a higher philosophy?" and thus indicate the true answer to be given, to which no words can do justice but your own:

> After all, is it not possible that we may find that everything has been necessarily produced; that all religions and superstitions, all mistakes and all crimes, were simply necessities? Is it not possible that out of this perception may come not only love and pity for others, but absolute justification for the individual? May we not find that every soul has, like Mazeppa, been lashed to the wild horse of passion, or like Prometheus to the rocks of fate?

If this be the end of all philosophy, it is equally the end of "all things." Not only does it make an end of us and of our hopes of futurity, but of all that makes the present life worth living — of all freedom, and hence of all virtue. There are no more any moral distinctions in the world — no good and no evil, no right and no wrong; nothing but grim necessity. With such a creed, I wonder how you can ever stand at the bar, and argue for the conviction of a criminal. Why should he be convicted and punished for what he could not help? Indeed he is not a criminal, since there is no such thing as crime. He is not to blame. Was he not "lashed to the wild horse of passion," carried away by a power beyond his control? What cruelty to thrust him behind iron bars! Poor fellow! he deserves our pity. Let us hasten to relieve him from a position which must be so painful, and make our humble apology for having presumed to punish him for an act in which he only obeyed an impulse which he could not resist. This will be "absolute justification for the individual." But what will become of society, you do not tell us.

Are you aware that in this last attainment of "a better, a higher philosophy" (which is simply absolute fatalism), you have swung round to the side of John Calvin, and gone far beyond him? That you, who have exhausted all the resources of the English language in denouncing his creed as the most horrible of human beliefs — brainless, soulless, heartless; who have held it up to scorn and derision; now hold to the blackest Calvinism that was ever taught by man? You cannot find words sufficient to express your horror of the doctrine of Divine decrees; and yet here you have decrees with a vengeance — predestination and damnation, both in one. Under such a creed, man is a thousand times worse off than under ours: for he has absolutely no hope. You may say that at any rate he cannot suffer forever. You do not know even that; but at any rate *he suffers as long as he exists.* There is no God above to show him pity, and grant him release; but as long as the ages roll, he is "lashed to the rocks of fate," with the insatiate vulture tearing at his heart!

In reading your glittering phrases, I seem to be losing hold of everything, and to be sinking, sinking, till I touch the lowest depths of an abyss; while from the blackness above me a sound like a death-knell tolls the midnight of the soul. If I believed this I should cry, God help us all! Or no — for there would be no God, and even this last consolation would be denied us: for why should we offer a prayer which can neither be heard nor answered? As well might we ask mercy from "the rocks of fate" to which we are chained forever!

Recoiling from this Gospel of Despair, I turn to One in whose face there is something at once human and divine — an indescribable majesty, united with more than human tenderness and pity; One who was born among the poor and had not where to lay His head, and yet went about doing good; poor, yet making many rich; who trod the world in deepest loneliness, and yet whose presence lighted up every dwelling into which He came; who took up little children in His arms, and blessed them; a giver of joy to others, and yet a sufferer himself; who tasted every human sorrow, and yet was always ready to minister to others' grief; weeping with them that wept; coming to Bethany to comfort Mary and Martha concerning their brother; rebuking the proud, but gentle and pitiful to the most abject of human creatures; stopping amid the throng at the cry of a blind beggar by the wayside; willing to be known as "the friend of sinners," if He might recall them into the way of peace; who did not scorn even the fallen woman who sank at His feet, but by His gentle word, "Neither do I condemn thee; go and sin no more," lifted her up, and set her in the path of a virtuous womanhood; and who, when dying on the cross, prayed: "Father, forgive them, for they know not what they do." In this Friend of the friendless, Comforter of the comfortless, Forgiver of the penitent, and Guide of the erring, I find a greatness that I had not found in any of the philosophers or teachers of the world. No voice in all the ages thrills me like that which whispers close to my heart, "Come unto me and I will give you rest," to which I answer: THIS IS MY MASTER, AND I WILL FOLLOW HIM.

Henry M. Field

Letter to Dr. Field

My Dear Mr. Field:

With great pleasure I have read your second letter, in which you seem to admit that men may differ even about religion without being responsible for that difference; that every man has the right to read the Bible for himself, state freely the conclusion at which he arrives, and that it is not only his privilege, but his duty to speak the truth; that Christians can hardly be happy in heaven, while those they loved on earth are suffering with the lost; that it is not a crime to investigate, to think, to reason, to observe, and to be governed by evidence; that credulity is not a virtue, and that the open mouth of ignorant wonder is not the only entrance to Paradise; that belief is not necessary to salvation, and that no man can justly be made to suffer eternal pain for having expressed an intellectual conviction.

You seem to admit that no man can justly be held responsible for his thoughts; that the brain thinks without asking our consent, and that we believe or disbelieve without an effort of the will.

I congratulate you upon the advance that you have made. You not only admit that we have the right to think, but that we have the right to express our honest thoughts. You admit that the Christian world no longer believes in the fagot, the dungeon, and the thumb-screw. Has the Christian world outgrown its God? Has man become more merciful than his maker? If man will not torture his fellow-man on account of a difference of opinion, will a God of infinite love torture one of his children for what is called the sin of unbelief? Has man outgrown the Inquisition, and will God forever be the warden of a penitentiary? The walls of the old dungeons have fallen, and light now visits the cell where brave men perished in darkness. Is Jehovah to keep the cells of perdition in repair forever, and are his children to be the eternal prisoners?

It seems hard for you to appreciate the mental condition of one who regards all gods as substantially the same; that is to say, who thinks of them all as myths and phantoms born of the imagination, — characters in the religious fictions of the race. To you it probably seems strange that a man should think far more of Jupiter than of Jehovah. Regarding them both as creations of the mind, I choose between them, and I prefer the God of the Greeks, on the same principle that I prefer Portia to Iago; and yet I regard them, one and all, as children of the imagination, as phantoms born of human fears and human hopes.

Surely nothing was further from my mind than to hurt the feelings of any one by speaking of the Presbyterian God. I simply intended to speak of the God of the Presbyterians. Certainly the God of the Presbyterian is not the God of the Catholic, nor is he the God of the Mohammedan or Hindoo. He is a special creation suited only to certain minds. These minds have naturally come together, and they form what we call the Presbyterian Church. As a matter of fact, no two Churches can by any possibility have precisely the same God; neither can any two human beings conceive of precisely the same Deity. In every man's God there is, to say the least, a part of that man. The lower the man, the lower his conception of God. The higher the man, the grander his Deity must be. The savage who adorns his body with a belt from which hang the scalps of enemies slain in battle, has no conception of a loving, of a forgiving God; his God, of necessity, must be as revengeful, as heartless, as infamous as the God of John Calvin.

You do not exactly appreciate my feeling. I do not hate Presbyterians; I hate Presbyterianism. I hate with all my heart the creed of that church, and I most heartily despise the God described in the Confession of Faith. But some of the best friends I have in the world are afflicted with the mental malady known as Presbyterianism. They are the victims of the consolation growing out of the belief that a vast majority of their fellow-men are doomed to suffer eternal torment, to the end that their Creator may be eternally glorified. I have said many times, and I say again, that I do not despise a man because he has the rheumatism; I despise the rheumatism because it has a man.

But I do not insist that the Presbyterians have assumed to appropriate to themselves their Supreme Being, and that they have claimed, and that they do claim, to be the "special objects of his favor." They do claim to be the very elect, and they do insist that God looks upon them as the objects of his special care. They do claim that the light of Nature, without the torch of the Presbyterian creed, is insufficient to guide any soul to the gate of heaven. They do insist that even those who never heard of Christ, or never heard of the God of the Presbyterians, will be eternally lost; and they not only claim this, but that their fate will illustrate not only the justice but the mercy of God. Not only so, but they insist that the morality of an unbeliever is displeasing to God, and that the love of an unconverted mother for her helpless child is nothing less than sin.

When I meet a man who really believes the Presbyterian creed, I think of the Laocoon. I feel as though looking upon a human being helpless in the coils of an immense and poisonous serpent. But I congratulate you with all my heart that you have repudiated this infamous, this savage creed; that you now admit that reason was given us to be exercised; that God will not torture any man for entertaining an honest doubt, and that in the world to come "every man will be judged according to the deeds done in the body."

Let me quote your exact language: "I believe that in the future world every man will be judged according to the deeds done in the body." Do you not see that you have bidden farewell to the Presbyterian Church? In that sentence you have thrown away the atonement, you have denied the efficacy of the blood of Jesus Christ, and you have denied the necessity of belief. If we are to be judged by the deeds done in the body, that is the end of the Presbyterian scheme of salvation. I sincerely congratulate you for having repudiated the savagery of Calvinism.

It also gave me great pleasure to find that you have thrown away, with a kind of glad shudder, that infamy of infamies, the dogma of eternal pain. I have denounced that inhuman belief; I have denounced every creed that had coiled within it that viper; I have denounced every man who preached it, the book that contains it, and with all my heart the God who threatens it; and at last I have the happiness of seeing the editor of the New York *Evangelist* admit that devout Christians do not believe that lie, and quote with approbation the words of a minister of the Church of England to the effect that all men will be finally recovered and made happy.

Do you find this doctrine of hope in the Presbyterian creed? Is this star, that sheds light on every grave, found in your Bible? Did Christ have in his mind the shining truth that all the children of men will at last be filled with joy, when he uttered these comforting words: "Depart from me, ye cursed, into everlasting fire prepared for the devil and his angels"? Do you find in this flame the bud of hope, or the flower of promise?

You suggest that it is possible that "the incurably bad will be annihilated," and you say that such a fate can have no terrors for me, as I look upon annihilation as the common lot of all. Let us examine this position. Why should a God of infinite wisdom create men and women whom he knew would be "incurably bad"? What would you say of a mechanic who was forced to destroy his own productions on the ground that they were "incurably bad"? Would you say that he was an infinitely wise mechanic? Does infinite justice annihilate the work of infinite wisdom? Does God, like an ignorant doctor, bury his mistakes?

Besides, what right have you to say that I "look upon annihilation as the common lot of all"? Was there any such thought in my Reply? Do you find it in any published words of mine? Do you find anything in what I have written tending to show that I believe in annihilation? Is it not true that I say now, and that I have always said, that I do not know? Does a lack of knowledge as to the fate of the human soul imply a belief in annihilation? Does it not equally imply a belief in immortality?

You have been — at least until recently — a believer in the inspiration of the Bible and in the truth of its every word. What do you say to the following: "For that which befalleth the sons of men befalleth beasts; even one thing befalleth them: as the one dieth, so dieth the other; yea, they have all one breath; so that a man hath no pre-eminence above a beast." You will see that the inspired writer is not satisfied with admitting that he does not know. "As the cloud is consumed and vanisheth away; so he that goeth down to the grave shall come up no more." Was it not cruel for an inspired man to attack a sacred belief?

You seem surprised that I should speak of the doctrine of eternal pain as "the black thunder-cloud that darkens all the horizon, casting its mighty shadows over the life that now is and that which is to come." If that doctrine be true, what else is there worthy of engaging the attention of the human mind? It is the blackness that extinguishes every star. It is the abyss in which every hope must perish. It leaves a universe without justice and without mercy — a future without one ray of light, and a present with nothing but fear. It makes heaven an impossibility, God an infinite monster, and man an eternal victim. Nothing can redeem a religion in which this dogma is found. Clustered about it are all the snakes of the Furies.

But you have abandoned this infamy, and you have admitted that we are to be judged according to the deeds done in the body. Nothing can be nearer self-evident than the fact that a finite being cannot commit an infinite sin; neither can a finite being do an infinitely good deed. That is to say, no one can deserve for any act eternal pain, and no one for any deed can deserve eternal joy. If we are to be judged by the deeds done in the body, the old orthodox hell and heaven both become impossible.

So, too, you have recognized the great and splendid truth that sin cannot be predicated on an intellectual conviction. This is the first great step toward the liberty of soul. You admit that there is no morality and no immorality in belief — that is to say, in the simple operation of the mind in weighing evidence, in observing facts, and in drawing conclusions. You admit that these things are without sin and without guilt. Had all men so believed there never could have been religious persecution — the Inquisition could not have been built, and the idea of eternal pain never could have polluted the human heart.

You have been driven to the passions for the purpose of finding what you are pleased to call "sin" and "responsibility"; and you say, speaking of a human being, "but if he is warped by passion so that he cannot see things truly, then is he responsible." One would suppose that the use of the word "cannot" is inconsistent with the idea of responsibility. What is passion? There are certain desires, swift, thrilling, that quicken the action of the heart — desires that fill the brain with blood, with fire and flame — desires that bear the same relation to judgment that storms and waves bear to the compass on a ship. Is passion necessarily produced? Is there an adequate cause for every effect? Can you by any possibility think of an effect without a cause, and can you by any possibility think of an effect that is not a cause, or can you think of a cause that is not an effect? Is not the history of real civilization the slow and gradual emancipation of the intellect, of the judgment, from the mastery of passion? Is not that man civilized whose reason sits the crowned monarch of his brain — whose passions are his servants?

Who knows the strength of the temptation to another? Who knows how little has been resisted by those who stand, how much has been resisted by those who fall? Who knows whether the victor or the victim made the braver and the more gallant fight? In judging of our fellow-men we must take into consideration the circumstances of ancestry, of race, of nationality, of employment, of opportunity, of education, and of the thousand influences that tend to mold or mar the character of man. Such a view is the mother of charity, and makes the God of the Presbyterians impossible.

At last you have seen the impossibility of forgiveness. That is to say, you perceive that after forgiveness the crime remains, and its children, called consequences, still live. You recognize the lack of philosophy in that doctrine. You still believe in what you call "the forgiveness of sins," but you admit that forgiveness cannot reverse the course of nature, and cannot prevent the operation of natural law. You also admit that if a man lives after death, he preserves his personal identity, his memory, and that the consequences of his actions will follow him through all the eternal years. You admit that consequences are immortal. After making this admission, of what use is the old idea of the forgiveness of sins? How can the criminal be washed clean and pure in the blood of another? In spite of this forgiveness, in spite of this blood, you have taken the ground that consequences, like the dogs of Actaeon, follow even a Presbyterian, even one of the elect, within the heavenly gates. If you wish to be logical, you must also admit that the consequences of good deeds, like winged angels, follow even the atheist within the gates of hell.

You have had the courage of your convictions, and you have said that we are to be judged according to the deeds done in the body. By that judgment I am willing to abide. But, whether willing or not, I must abide, because there is no power, no God that can step between me and the consequences of my acts. I wish no heaven that I have not earned, no happiness to which I am not entitled. I do not wish to become an immortal pauper; neither am I willing to extend unworthy hands for alms.

My dear Mr. Field, you have outgrown your creed — as every Presbyterian must who grows at all. You are far better than the spirit of the Old Testament; far better, in my judgment, even than the spirit of the New. The creed that you have left behind, that you have repudiated, teaches that a man may be guilty of every crime — that he may have driven his wife to insanity, that his example may have led his children to the penitentiary, or to the gallows, and that yet, at the eleventh hour, he may, by what is called "repentance," be washed absolutely pure by the blood of another and receive and wear upon his brow the laurels of eternal peace. Not only so, but that creed has taught that this wretch in heaven could look back on the poor earth and see the wife, whom he swore to love and cherish, in the mad-house, surrounded by imaginary serpents, struggling in the darkness of night, made insane by his heartlessness — that creed has taught and teaches that he could look back and see his children in prison cells, or on the scaffold with the noose about their necks, and that these visions would not bring a shade of sadness to his redeemed and happy face. It is this doctrine, it is this dogma — so bestial, so savage as to beggar all the languages of men — that I have denounced. All the words of hatred, loathing and contempt, found in all the dialects and tongues of men, are not sufficient to express my hatred, my contempt, and my loathing of this creed.

You say that it is impossible for you not to believe in the existence of God. With this statement, I find no fault. Your mind is so that a belief in the existence of a Supreme Being gives satisfaction and content. Of course, you are entitled to no credit for this belief, as you ought not to be rewarded for believing that which you cannot help believing; neither should I be punished for failing to believe that which I cannot believe.

You believe because you see in the world around you such an adaptation of means to ends that you are satisfied there is design. I admit that when Robinson Crusoe saw in the sand the print of a human foot, like and yet unlike his own, he was justified in drawing the conclusion that a human being had been there. The inference was drawn from his own experience, and was within the scope of his own mind. But I do not agree with you that he "knew" a human being had been there; he had only sufficient evidence upon which to found a belief. He did not know the footsteps of all animals; he could not have known that no animal except man could have made that footprint. In order to have known that it was the foot of man, he must have known that no other animal was capable of making it, and he must have known that no other being had produced in the sand the likeness of this human foot.

You see what you call evidences of intelligence in the universe, and you draw the conclusion that there must be an infinite intelligence. Your conclusion is far wider than your premise. Let us suppose, as Mr. Hume supposed, that there is a pair of scales, one end of which is in darkness, and you find that a pound weight, or a ten-pound weight, placed upon that end of the scale in the light is raised; have you the right to say that there is an infinite weight on the end in darkness, or are you compelled to say only that there is weight enough on the end in darkness to raise the weight on the end in light?

It is illogical to say, because of the existence of this earth and of what you can see in and about it, that there must be an infinite intelligence. You do not know that even the creation of this world, and of all planets discovered, required an infinite power, or infinite wisdom. I admit that it is impossible for me to look at a watch and draw the inference that there was no design in its construction, or that it only happened. I could not regard it as a product of some freak of nature, neither could I imagine that its various parts were brought together and set in motion by chance. I am not a believer in chance. But there is a vast difference between what man has made and the materials of which he has constructed the things he has made. You find a watch, and you say that it exhibits, or shows design. You insist that it is so wonderful it must have had a designer — in other words, that it is too wonderful not to have been constructed. You then find the watchmaker, and you say with regard to him that he too must have had a designer, for he is more wonderful than the watch. In imagination you go from the watchmaker to the being you call God, and you say he designed the watchmaker, but he himself was not designed because he is too wonderful to have been designed. And yet in the case of the watch and of the watchmaker, it was the wonder that suggested design, while in the case of the maker of the watchmaker the wonder denied a designer. Do you not see that this argument devours itself? If wonder suggests a designer, can it go on increasing until it denies that which it suggested?

You must remember, too, that the argument of design is applicable to all. You are not at liberty to stop at sunrise and sunset and growing corn and all that adds to the happiness of man; you must go further. You must admit that an infinitely wise and merciful God designed the fangs of serpents, the machinery by which the poison is distilled, the ducts by which it is carried to the fang, and that the same intelligence impressed this serpent with a desire to deposit this deadly virus in the flesh of man. You must believe that an infinitely wise God so constructed this world, that in the process of cooling, earthquakes would be caused — earthquakes that devour and overwhelm cities and states. Do you see any design in the volcano that sends its rivers of lava over the fields and the homes of men? Do you really think a perfectly good being designed the invisible parasites that infest the air, that inhabit the water, and that finally attack and destroy the health and life of man? Do you see the same design in cancers that you do in wheat and corn? Did God invent tumors for the brain? Was it his ingenuity that so designed the human race that millions of people should be born deaf and dumb, that millions should be idiotic? Did he knowingly plant in the blood or brain the seeds of insanity? Did he cultivate those seeds? Do you see any design in this?

Man calls that good which increases his happiness, and that evil which gives him pain. In the olden time, back of the good he placed a God; back of the evil a devil; but now the orthodox world is driven to admit that the God is the author of all.

For my part, I see no goodness in the pestilence — no mercy in the bolt that leaps from the cloud and leaves the mark of death on the breast of a loving mother. I see no generosity in famine, no goodness in disease, no mercy in want and agony. And yet you say that the being who created parasites that live only by inflicting pain — the being responsible for all the sufferings of mankind — you say that he has "a tenderness compared to which all human love is faint and cold." Yet according to the doctrine of the orthodox world, this being of infinite love and tenderness so created nature that its light misleads, and left a vast majority of the human race to blindly grope their way to endless pain.

You insist that a knowledge of God — a belief in God — is the foundation of social order; and yet this God of infinite tenderness has left for thousands and thousands of years nearly all of his children without a revelation. Why should infinite goodness leave the existence of God in doubt? Why should he see millions in savagery destroying the lives of each other, eating the flesh of each other, and keep his existence a secret from man? Why did he allow the savages to depend on sunrise and sunset and clouds? Why did he leave this great truth to a few half-crazed prophets, or to a cruel, heartless and ignorant church? The sentence "There is a God" could have been imprinted on every blade of grass, on every leaf, on every star. An infinite God has no excuse for leaving his children in doubt and darkness.

There is still another point. You know that for thousands of ages men worshiped wild beasts as God. You know that for countless generations they knelt by coiled serpents, believing those serpents to be gods. Why did the real God secrete himself and allow his poor, ignorant, savage children to imagine that he was a beast, a serpent? Why did this God allow mothers to sacrifice their babes? Why did he not emerge from the darkness? Why did he not say to the poor mother, "Do not sacrifice your babe; keep it in your arms; press it to your bosom; let it be the solace of your declining years. I take no delight in the death of children; I am not what you suppose me to be; I am not a beast; I am not a serpent; I am full of love and kindness and mercy, and I want my children to be happy in this world"? Did the God who allowed a mother to sacrifice her babe through the mistaken idea that he, the God, demanded the sacrifice, feel a tenderness toward that mother "compared to which all human love is faint and cold"? Would a good father allow some of his children to kill others of his children to please him?

There is still another question. Why should God, a being of infinite tenderness, leave the question of immortality in doubt? How is it that there is nothing in the Old Testament on this subject? Why is it that he who made all the constellations did not put in his heaven the star of hope? How do you account for the fact that you do not find in the Old Testament, from the first mistake in Genesis, to the last curse in Malachi, a funeral service? Is it not strange that some one in the Old Testament did not stand by an open grave of father or mother and say: "We shall meet again"? Was it because the divinely inspired men did not know?

You taunt me by saying that I know no more of the immortality of the soul than Cicero knew. I admit it. I know no more than the lowest savage, no more than a doctor of divinity — that is to say, nothing.

Is it not, however, a curious fact that there is less belief in the immortality of the soul in Christian countries than in heathen lands — that the belief in immortality, in an orthodox church, is faint and cold and speculative, compared with that belief in India, in China, or in the Pacific Isles? Compare the belief in immortality in America, of Christians, with that of the followers of Mohammed. Do not Christians weep above their dead? Does a belief in immortality keep back their tears? After all, the promises are so far away, and the dead are so near — the echoes of words said to have been spoken more than eighteen centuries ago are lost in the sounds of the clods that fall on the coffin. And yet, compared with the orthodox hell, compared with the prison-house of God, how ecstatic is the grave — the grave without a sigh, without a tear, without a dream, without a fear. Compared with the immortality promised by the Presbyterian creed, how beautiful annihilation seems. To be nothing — how much better than to be a convict forever. To be unconscious dust — how much better than to be a heartless angel.

There is not, there never has been, there never will be, any consolation in orthodox Christianity. It offers no consolation to any good and loving man. I prefer the consolation of Nature, the consolation of hope, the consolation springing from human affection. I prefer the simple desire to live and love forever.

Of course, it would be a consolation to know that we have an "Almighty Friend" in heaven; but an "Almighty Friend" who cares nothing for us, who allows us to be stricken by his lightning, frozen by his winter, starved by his famine, and at last imprisoned in his hell, is a friend I do not care to have.

I remember "the poor slave mother who sat alone in her cabin, having been robbed of her children:" and, my dear Mr. Field, I also remember that the people who robbed her justified the robbery by reading passages from the sacred Scriptures. I remember that while the mother wept, the robbers, some of whom were Christians, read this: "Buy of the heathen round about, and they shall be your bondmen and bondwomen forever." I remember, too, that the robbers read: "Servants be obedient unto your masters;" and they said, this passage is the only message from the heart of God to the scarred back of the slave. I remember this, and I remember, also, that the poor slave mother upon her knees in wild and wailing accents called on the "Almighty Friend," and I remember that her prayer was never heard, and that her sobs died in the negligent air.

You ask me whether I would "rob this poor woman of such a friend?" My answer is this: I would give her liberty; I would break her chains. But let me ask you, did an "Almighty Friend" see the woman he loved "with a tenderness compared to which all human love is faint and cold," and the woman who loved him, robbed of her children? What was the "Almighty Friend" worth to her? She preferred her babe.

How could the "Almighty Friend" see his poor children pursued by hounds — his children whose only crime was the love of liberty — how could he see that, and take sides with the hounds? Do you believe that the "Almighty Friend" then governed the world? Do you really think that he "Bade the slave-ship speed from coast to coast, Fanned by the wings of the Holy Ghost"?

Do you believe that the "Almighty Friend" saw all of the tragedies that were enacted in the jungles of Africa — that he watched the wretched slave-ships, saw the miseries of the middle passages, heard the blows of all the whips, saw all the streams of blood, all the agonized faces of women, all the tears that were shed? Do you believe that he saw and knew all these things, and that he, the "Almighty Friend," looked coldly down and stretched no hand to save?

You persist, however, in endeavoring to account for the miseries of the world by taking the ground that happiness is not the end of life. You say that "the real end of life is character, and that no discipline can be too severe which leads us to suffer and be strong." Upon this subject you use the following language: "If you could have your way you would make everybody happy; there would be no more poverty, and no more sickness or pain." And this you say, is a "child's picture, hardly worthy of a stalwart man." Let me read you another "child's picture," which you will find in the twenty-first chapter of Revelation, supposed to have been written by St. John, the Divine: "And I heard a great voice out of heaven saying, behold the tabernacle of God is with men, and he will dwell with them, and they shall be his people, and God himself shall be with them, and be their God; and God shall wipe away all tears from their eyes, and there shall be no more death, neither sorrow, nor crying, neither shall there be any more pain."

If you visited some woman living in a tenement, supporting by her poor labor a little family — a poor woman on the edge of famine, sewing, it may be, her eyes blinded by tears — would you tell her that "the world is not a playground in which men are to be petted and indulged like children"? Would you tell her that to think of a world without poverty, without tears, without pain, is "a child's picture"? If she asked you for a little assistance, would you refuse it on the ground that by being helped she might lose character? Would you tell her: "God does not wish to have you happy; happiness is a very foolish end; character is what you want, and God has put you here with these helpless, starving babes, and he has put this burden on your young life simply that you may suffer and be strong. I would help you gladly, but I do not wish to defeat the plans of your Almighty Friend"? You can reason one way, but you would act the other.

I agree with you that work is good, that struggle is essential; that men are made manly by contending with each other and with the forces of nature; but there is a point beyond which struggle does not make character; there is a point at which struggle becomes failure.

Can you conceive of an "Almighty Friend" deforming his children because he loves them? Did he allow the innocent to languish in dungeons because he was their friend? Did he allow the noble to perish upon the scaffold, the great and the self-denying to be burned at the stake, because he had the power to save? Was he restrained by love? Did this "Almighty Friend" allow millions of his children to be enslaved to the end that the "splendor of virtue might have a dark background"? You insist that "suffering patiently borne, is a means of the greatest elevation of character, and in the end of the highest enjoyment." Do you not then see that your "Almighty Friend" has been unjust to the happy — that he is cruel to those whom we call the fortunate — that he is indifferent to the men who do not suffer — that he leaves all the happy and prosperous and joyous without character, and that in the end, according to your doctrine, they are the losers?

But, after all, there is no need of arguing this question further. There is one fact that destroys forever your theory — and that is the fact that millions upon millions die in infancy. Where do they get "elevation of character"? What opportunity is given to them to "suffer and be strong"? Let us admit that we do not know. Let us say that the mysteries of life, of good and evil, of joy and pain, have never been explained. Is character of no importance in heaven? How is it possible for angels, living in "a child's picture," to "suffer and be strong"? Do you not see that, according to your philosophy, only the damned can grow great — only the lost can become sublime?

You do not seem to understand what I say with regard to what I call the higher philosophy. When that philosophy is accepted, of course there will be good in the world, there will be evil, there will still be right and wrong. What is good? That which tends to the happiness of sentient beings. What is evil? That which tends to the misery, or tends to lessen the happiness of sentient beings. What is right? The best thing to be done under the circumstances — that is to say, the thing that will increase or preserve the happiness of man. What is wrong? That which tends to the misery of man.

What you call liberty, choice, morality, responsibility, have nothing whatever to do with this. There is no difference between necessity and liberty. He who is free, acts from choice. What is the foundation of his choice? What we really mean by liberty is freedom from personal dictation — we do not wish to be controlled by the will of others. To us the nature of things does not seem to be a master — Nature has no will.

Society has the right to protect itself by imprisoning those who prey upon its interests; but it has no right to punish. It may have the right to destroy the life of one dangerous to the community; but what has freedom to do with this? Do you kill the poisonous serpent because he knew better than to bite? Do you chain a wild beast because he is morally responsible? Do you not think that the criminal deserves the pity of the virtuous?

I was looking forward to the time when the individual might feel justified — when the convict who had worn the garment of disgrace might know and feel that he had acted as he must.

There is an old Hindoo prayer to which I call your attention: "Have mercy, God, upon the vicious; Thou hast already had mercy upon the just by making them just."

Is it not possible that we may find that everything has been necessarily produced? This, of course, would end in the justification of men. Is not that a desirable thing? Is it not possible that intelligence may at last raise the human race to that sublime and philosophic height?

You insist, however, that this is Calvinism. I take it for granted that you understand Calvinism — but let me tell you what it is. Calvinism asserts that man does as he must, and that, notwithstanding this fact, he is responsible for what he does — that is to say, for what he is compelled to do — that is to say, for what God does with him; and that, for doing that which he must, an infinite God, who compelled him to do it, is justified in punishing the man in eternal fire; this, not because the man ought to be damned, but simply for the glory of God.

Starting from the same declaration, that man does as he must, I reach the conclusion that we shall finally perceive in this fact justification for every individual. And yet you see no difference between my doctrine and Calvinism. You insist that damnation and justification are substantially the same; and yet the difference is as great as human language can express. You call the justification of all the world "the Gospel of Despair," and the damnation of nearly all the human race the "Consolation of Religion."

After all, my dear friend, do you not see that when you come to speak of that which is really good, you are compelled to describe your ideal human being? It is the human in Christ, and only the human, that you by any possibility can understand. You speak of one who was born among the poor, who went about doing good, who sympathized with those who suffered. You have described, not only one, but many millions of the human race. Millions of others have carried light to those sitting in darkness; millions and millions have taken children in their arms; millions have wept that those they love might smile. No language can express the goodness, the heroism, the patience and self-denial of the many millions, dead and living, who have preserved in the family of man the jewels of the heart. You have clad one being in all the virtues of the race, in all the attributes of gentleness, patience, goodness, and love, and yet that being, according to the New Testament, had to his character another side. True, he said, "Come unto me and I will give you rest;" but what did he say to those who failed to come? You pour out your whole heart in thankfulness to this one man who suffered for the right, while I thank not only this one, but all the rest. My heart goes out to all the great, the self-denying and the good, — to the founders of nations, singers of songs, builders of homes; to the inventors, to the artists who have filled the world with beauty, to the composers of music, to the soldiers of the right, to the makers of mirth, to honest men, and to all the loving mothers of the race.

Compare, for one moment, all that the Savior did, all the pain and suffering that he relieved, — compare all this with the discovery of anæsthetics. Compare your prophets with the inventors, your Apostles with the Keplers, the Humboldts and the Darwins.

I belong to the great church that holds the world within its starlit aisles; that claims the great and good of every race and clime; that finds with joy the grain of gold in every creed, and floods with light and love the germs of good in every soul.

Most men are provincial, narrow, one sided, only partially

developed. In a new country we often see a little patch of land, a clearing in which the pioneer has built his cabin. This little clearing is just large enough to support a family, and the remainder of the farm is still forest, in which snakes crawl and wild beasts occasionally crouch. It is thus with the brain of the average man. There is a little clearing, a little patch, just large enough to practice medicine with, or sell goods, or practice law; or preach with, or do some kind of business, sufficient to obtain bread and food and shelter for a family, while all the rest of the brain is covered with primeval forest, in which lie coiled the serpents of superstition and from which spring the wild beasts of orthodox religion.

Neither in the interest of truth, nor for the benefit of man, is it necessary to assert what we do not know. No cause is great enough to demand a sacrifice of candor. The mysteries of life and death, of good and evil, have never yet been solved.

I combat those only who, knowing nothing of the future, prophesy an eternity of pain — those only who sow the seeds of fear in the hearts of men — those only who poison all the springs of life, and seat a skeleton at every feast.

Let us banish the shriveled hags of superstition; let us welcome the beautiful daughters of truth and joy.

Robert G. Ingersoll

"AIMS AND PURPOSES"

(as recorded in documents of incorporation)

AMERICAN ATHEISTS ARE ORGANIZED:

(1) to stimulate and promote freedom of thought and inquiry concerning religious beliefs, creeds, dogmas, tenets, rituals, and practices;

(2) to collect and disseminate information, data, and literature on all religions and promote a more thorough understanding of them, their origins, and their histories;

(3) to advocate, labor for, and promote in all lawful ways the complete and absolute separation of state and church;

(4) to advocate, labor for, and promote in all lawful ways the establishment and maintenance of a thoroughly secular system of education available to all;

(5) to encourage the development and public acceptance of a humane ethical system, stressing the mutual sympathy, understanding, and interdependence of all people and the corresponding responsibility of each individual in relation to society;

(6) to develop and propagate a social philosophy in which man is the central figure, who alone must be the source of strength, progress, and ideals for the well-being and happiness of humanity;

(7) to promote the study of the arts and sciences and of all problems affecting the maintenance, perpetuation, and enrichment of human (and other) life; and

(8) to engage in such social, educational, legal, and cultural activity as will be useful and beneficial to members of American Atheists and to society as a whole.

"DEFINITIONS"

Atheism is the *Weltanschauung* (comprehensive conception of the world and of total human life value systems) of persons who are *free* from theism — *i.e.*, free *from* religion. It is predicated on ancient Greek Materialism.

American Atheism may be defined as the mental attitude that unreservedly accepts the supremacy of reason and aims at establishing a life-style and ethical outlook verifiable by experience and the scientific method, independent of all arbitrary assumptions of authority or creeds.

Materialism declares that the cosmos is devoid of immanent conscious purpose; that it is governed by its own inherent, immutable, and impersonal laws; that there is no supernatural interference in human life; that man — finding his resources within himself — can and must create his own destiny. Materialism restores to man his dignity and his intellectual integrity. It teaches that we must prize our life on earth and strive always to improve it. It holds that man is capable of creating a social system based on reason and justice. Materialism's "faith" is in man and man's ability to transform the world culture by his own efforts. This is a commitment which is in every essence life-asserting. It considers the struggle for progress as a moral obligation and impossible without noble ideas that inspire man to struggle and bold creative works. Materialism holds that humankind's potential for good and for an outreach to more fulfilling cultural development is, for all practical purposes, unlimited.

American Atheists is a nonpolitical, nonprofit, educational organization. Another of its functions is to act as a "watchdog" to challenge any attempted breach of what Thomas Jefferson called "the wall of separation between state and church," upon which principle our nation was founded.

Membership is open only to those who are in accord with the "Aims and Purposes" indicated above and who are Atheist Materialists. Membership in the national organization is a prerequisite for membership in state, county, city, or local chapters. Membership fee categories are reflected on the reverse side of this sheet (American Atheists Membership Application form).

A complete copy of the Constitution and By-Laws of American Atheists is available upon request. Send $1.00 for postage and handling to:

Constitution and By-Laws
American Atheists, Inc.
P.O. Box 140195
Austin, TX 78714-0195

Membership Application For American Atheists

Last name: ______________________ First name: ______________________

Companion's name (if family or couple membership)

Last name: ______________________ First name: ______________________

Address ____

City/State/Zip ____

This is to certify that I am/we are in agreement with the "Aims and Purposes"* and the "Definitions"* of American Atheists. I/we consider myself/ourselves to be Materialist or Non-theist (*i.e.*, A-theist) and I/we have, therefore, a particular interest in the separation of state and church and American Atheists' efforts on behalf of that principle.

I/we usually identify myself/ourselves for public purposes as (check one):

- ☐ Atheist
- ☐ Freethinker
- ☐ Humanist
- ☐ Rationalist
- ☐ Objectivist
- ☐ Ethical Culturalist
- ☐ Unitarian
- ☐ Secularist
- ☐ Agnostic
- ☐ Realist
- ☐ I/we evade any reply to a query
- ☐ Other: ______________________________

I am/we are, however, an Atheist(s) and I/we hereby make application for membership in American Atheists. Both dues and contributions are to a tax-exempt organization and I/we may claim these amounts as tax deductions on my/our income tax return(s). *(This application must be dated and signed by the applicant(s) to be accepted.)*

Signature ______________________________ Date ______________

Signature ______________________________ Date ______________

Membership in American Atheists includes a subscription to the monthly journal *American Atheist* and the monthly "Insider's Newsletter" as well as all the other rights and privileges of membership. Please indicate your choice of membership dues:

- ☐ Life, $500
- ☐ Couple Life, $750 (Please give both names above.)
- ☐ Sustaining, $100/year
- ☐ Couple/Family, $50/year (Please give all names above.)
- ☐ Individual, $40/year
- ☐ Age 65 or over, $20/year (Photocopy of ID required.)
- ☐ Unemployed, $20/year
- ☐ Student, $12/year (Photocopy of ID required.)

Upon your acceptance into membership, you will receive a handsome gold embossed membership card, a membership certificate personally signed by Jon G. Murray, president of American Atheists, our special monthly "Insider's Newsletter" to keep you informed of the activities of American Atheists, and a subscription to *American Atheist*. Life members receive a specially embossed pen and pencil set; sustaining members receive a commemorative pen. Your name will be sent to the chapter in your local area if there currently is one, and you will be contacted so you may become a part of the many local activities. Memberships and subscriptions are nonrefundable.

☐ I am/we are enclosing a check or money order for $ ____________ payable to: American Atheists

☐ Please charge my/our charge card for $ __________. ☐ Visa or ☐ Mastercard

Card # ______________________________

Bank No./Letters ______________________________

Expiration date: ______________________________

Signature ______________________________

Return form to:

American Atheists, Inc., P.O. Box 140195, Austin, TX 78714-0195